"*The Wizard behind the CEO* is as smart, quick, and hu
Linda McFarland. In this book, Linda takes us on a live
personal experiences, which teaches everything from w
need to have in common, to how to pull through with ¿
best laid plans are crashing around you. *The Wizard behind the CEO* provides
an abundance of eye-opening tips on how to 'wow' your manager during the
good times and the OMG! times. Linda creates a fabulously entertaining read!
Whether you're a newbie to the profession or a seasoned assistant, this book is
for you."

~ Nancy Nordberg, CEAP Certified, Executive Assistant to President & CEO

"Hold on to your hat! The true stories in this book will take you on a wild ride
and give you a rare glimpse into the intense world of Silicon Valley. Linda
shares her experiences in vivid detail and from the heart, providing valuable
insights into the enormous challenges, and sometimes ridiculous demands, of
being a world-class assistant. Funny? Of course! Because humor is a wonderful
way to maintain our perspective in the face of seemingly impossible challenges.
Enjoy!"

~ Kimberly Wiefling, Author of *Scrappy Project
Management*, Cofounder of Silicon Valley Alliances

"Linda, you are my SHERO! No matter what situation you find yourself in—
albeit language barriers, no plane, no lunch, no shuttle, no email—you just put
on your 'nothing can stop me' cape and jump over tall buildings in a single
bound!"

~ Lisa Milanes, Executive Assistant

"Being new to the assistant world, I found this book to be exactly the kind
of guidance and motivation I needed to grow in my career. Linda's stories
will resonate with anyone who has worked as an assistant, and they will leave
you feeling empowered to apply some of her lessons learned down the road.
Linda makes you realize you're not the only one who has dealt with some truly
enraging, complicated, and at times downright hilarious situations. Best of all,
Linda shows that being bold, getting creative, and having a sense of humor are
the special sauce to our magic touch."

~ Mandy King Massa, Executive Assistant

"As an assistant to a CEO, who continually strives to develop my skills and has been challenged to find material that truly speaks to my role, I was pleasantly surprised with the *Wizard*'s content. The book speaks to several situations I have encountered, such as the 'Mind-Reader Expectations' and 'The Case of the Missing Email.' I am comforted to know I am not the only one with an exciting role! I enjoyed finding scenarios I have yet to encounter, such as 'Murphy's Law and the Special Visa' and 'Adventures in Germany.' Going forward, I will be diligent when dealing with complex international matters. 'The Goose Coach' expressed the perfect sentiment for what team support looks like and what can be accomplished as a team."

~ Lisa Taylor, CEO Assistant

"What a wonderful read! *The Wizard behind the CEO* is full of practical, memorable advice, especially when it comes to turning stressful situations into successful outcomes. It's also a whole lot of fun!"

~ Susan Henley Spreitzer, CAP, OM, CAW

"How can one learn to create order in the C-Suite office and positively influence culture, all while remaining unfailingly calm? *The Wizard behind the CEO* guides the way through true stories from the trenches, which conclude with actionable tips and guidance. With humor, compassion, and discipline, Linda imparts her wisdom to help assistants seeking to strengthen their craft. Throughout her impressive career, Linda has conquered countless unbelievable adversities and generously shares how any assistant can do the same. This should be required reading for all assistants."

~ Ashley Griffin, Chief of Staff

"Linda has done it again! A perfect read for all admins, but be forewarned, you will not be able to put it down! Using humor and insight, as only Linda can, she illustrates the world of admins, and you will find yourself thinking, 'Yes! Yes!' as you relate to each story! The lessons learned at the end of each tale are motivational and pure gold! This book is a must-read for all admins and their executives!"

~ Cheryl Paul, Executive Assistant

"This book is a must-have and 'go to' whether you're in the realm of the administrative profession or elsewhere. The stories and related lessons apply to the everyday professional."

~ Jeanne Corsick, Executive Assistant

"Whether you're just starting your career or are a seasoned assistant, this is an outstanding book. Linda has demonstrated through sharing her amazing career stories that we are not alone and offered very good advice. I am inspired by her magical moments and appreciative of the WAND [What Assistants Need Daily] advice. We are only human after all. It is a reminder of how important it is to network and mentor."

~ Kathleen Robinson, Executive Assistant

"This is not just another book full of 'stories.' As I read Linda's experiences, I could hear the 'I can do this' emotion in her writing. The quotes that are added to each lesson speak to us as if they've been written with an admin's experience. I also enjoyed the learning bullets at the end of each story. Linda has a lot of knowledge and experience as a C-level assistant, and I appreciate that she is sharing it with the masses. This book is a great tool for any assistant at any level."

~ Kathy Cannon, Executive Assistant

"Linda's book will benefit you whether you are new to the administrative field or are an experienced CEO's assistant with more than 20 years. Real-life examples highlight challenges that we all face at some point. The magical wand with lessons learned at the end of each story emphasizes tricks and tips, which help us become more polished and make our jobs easier. Reminders to 'take a deep breath, keep our feet paddling underwater like crazy, while everything above water is calm' is just one of the alliterations used by Linda to help lock the lessons in our memories. I HIGHLY RECOMMEND THIS BOOK."

~ Lisa Buck, Director Administrative Services

"Thank you, Linda, for being such an inspiration to all of us. Your integrity, perseverance, and passion helped you navigate each situation in a positive, calm, professional manner with a wave of your wand to make the magic appear and bring calmness to chaos."

~ Sue Allen, Sr. Executive Assistant

"Linda's experiences will inspire you to communicate. It is a common message throughout her book. The little nuggets after each story—WAND—one doesn't find in a classroom. The value of the WAND is priceless. Assistants will embrace the challenges because the rewards are immense."

~ Marie Simmons, CEO Assistant

"I ABSOLUTELY loved this book! So many of the stories had me in stitches, and others were funny memories of similar snafus in my own professional life as an assistant. With the takeaways at the end of each story, this book provides valuable information for newer admins and great reminders for senior assistants. The tips and takeaways are great for both admins and their executives!"

~ Kelsey Mendenhall, Executive Assistant

"Linda IS magic! She is TOP in her field, an incredible coach and mentor, and one of the most bewitching storytellers. She can make you laugh, blink in disbelief, and sometimes wonder how this can all be possible! Linda is charm and elegance. She is real, she is approachable, and she is sharing all of this for the enlightenment of others. A totally enchanting experience."

~ MGS Keller, Music and Relationship Coach

"It takes not one but two successful business leaders to move a company forward! Linda demonstrates this in a fun and informative way, page after page in *The Wizard behind the CEO*. This gem brings to life the many skills needed to be successful in today's rapidly changing work environment: resourcefulness, grit, and competency, to name only a few. This is a must-read for every assistant who has found themselves in unimaginable situations or is eager to learn."

~ Sunny Nunan, Founder & CEO, The Admin Awards:
Celebrating Administrative Excellence

THE
Wizard
BEHIND THE CEO

Steve –
You are a
Finance wizard!
So glad I landed
in this role so
I could learn from
you! Best,
Linda
McFarland

Enchanted stories from the
assistant with the magic WAND

LINDA McFARLAND

Copyright © 2018 by Linda McFarland

Ascend2Success
2010 El Camino Real, Suite #510
Santa Clara, CA 95050
linda@ascend2success
www.thewizardbehindtheceo.com

ISBN-13: 978-1-7323995-0-1

Editing by Author One Stop (www.AuthorOneStop.com)
Design and production by Backspace Ink (www.backspaceink.com)

iStock's "Wizard Hat Magic Wand Star Drawing" by FrankRamspott
Back cover photo by Portraits by Rebecca (www.portraitsbyrebecca.com)

You can read more stories in my first book, *Sitting on a File Cabinet, Naked, with a Gun: True Stories of Silicon Valley CEO Assistants*, coauthored with Joanne Linden, available on Amazon.

I dedicate this book to my admin friends and mentors who encouraged me to share my stories, helped me financially (publishing costs money), and attended my workshops, events, and conferences. They reminded me of stories I had shared in the past. They listened, showed respect, shared their own stories, had confidence in me, and cheered me on. The list of names is too long. You all know who you are.

TABLE OF CONTENTS

TABLE OF CONTENTS

Foreword

When Linda told me that she was publishing her second book and asked if I'd be willing to write the foreword, I didn't hesitate. Linda and I worked together for four years, and she was a truly trusted business partner. She represented me and my role as chief executive officer (CEO) extraordinarily well, without abusing or improperly leveraging the "power of the office."

Linda is smart and empathetic with a mindset of "organization first" without selfish objectives. I could always count on her to be available and not intrusive. She was trusted by me, my executive staff, our board of directors, and her peers, and amazed me with how well she anticipated and managed details without coming across as a micromanager.

The culture of the company was very important to me. Linda learned and incorporated my style and helped us develop the right "tone at the top."

Another quality that I appreciated about Linda was her ability to keep her composure. Not only was she amazingly calm in chaos, she helped me as well. During my multiyear commute from Orange County to Silicon Valley, she greatly helped me integrate my professional and personal lives.

Linda has a great appreciation for her profession, and this book is another avenue for her to pay it forward. She is truly a wizard, and I found *The Wizard behind the CEO* a wonderful and insightful book full of challenges, successes, and yes, failures, of a rich career.

This book is a great way to learn from a role model and hopefully employ great insight and avoid the potential pitfalls we all face in our hectic business and personal lives. Each chapter contains stories that are not only delightful to read but each is followed by some excellent suggestions dubbed the WAND (What Assistants Need Daily). This magical advice frankly is relevant for not just assistants but their managers and indeed professionals in general who need to work together to accomplish goals.

I highly recommend this book for not only all assistants but also leaders who want to leverage their capabilities by working in close partnership with their assistant.

Linda has magically found ways to adapt to the CEOs she has supported over the years to achieve respect and success in her career. *Truly magical.*

~ Jeff Rodek, former Chairman and CEO, Hyperion

Acknowledgments

It takes great mentors, family, and friends to write a book. More importantly, it takes people who believe in you and want to see you succeed.

A special thank-you to the many CEOs (over a dozen) and other executives whom I've supported over the years. Little did they know at the time that some of our adventures would be published in a book! A few of you knew that might be the case and were willing to hire me anyway. Most of the stories are positive, although I do share my failures too. Thank you for taking a chance on me, believing in me, and providing me with opportunities to professionally learn and grow.

Last, but not least, is my amazing husband Tim McFarland. When I announced that I was writing Book #2, he didn't run away and hide. He reminded me of stories that he remembered me sharing, listened to many versions, and even provided honest input that sometimes challenged me to accept criticism to grow. His support didn't stop there. He has accompanied me to speaking engagements and networking and book events, and endured my preparation for administrative events, conferences, workshops, and so much more. Tim, thank you for being the love of my life; my friend; my biggest fan; a fabulous husband, father, and cherished grandfather; and someone who has not only believed in me but helped me accomplish the work that drives my passion for the administrative role.

Introduction

The Wizard behind the CEO: Enchanted stories from the assistant with the magic WAND is all about my adventures as an assistant. I've supported over a dozen CEOs in Silicon Valley—each one unique. I haven't had the opportunity to support a woman CEO, although my career isn't over yet!

Being a CEO assistant has incredible challenges. It takes good judgment, implausible instincts, confidentiality and discretion, an eye for detail, adaptability, resilience, proficient computer skills, the ability to anticipate instincts, problem-solving skills, meeting and event planner skills, a calm demeanor, resourcefulness, the ability to build lasting relationships with ease, an understanding of timing when it comes to delivering a critical message, negotiating skills, the desire to constantly learn, an understanding of an executive's business priorities and goals, and so much more. All these attributes together create the magic that assistants perform daily.

As I thought about the title for this book, I realized how much an assistant's position is like a wizard. A wizard is a person with magical powers, exceptional or extraordinary abilities, or a high standing with an organization. Wizards fear few things and are equal to most of them. They appear when least expected and bend things to their will. Wizards foretell without apparatus. They can be mysterious and amazing and do magical things with the wave of a wand. These are all attributes and characteristics of the assistant. I've seen dozens of assistants wave their magic wand and do unbelievable things behind the scenes to make things happen *magically* for a seamless, flowing event or meeting.

Each story includes valuable lessons learned and techniques to help assistants make better decisions. I refer to them as WAND (What Assistants Need Daily). We all need ideas to help us do our job better and keep us relevant and productive.

I hope you'll find the stories humorous and occasionally moving and enjoy the surprises along the way. They reveal how an ordinary human being empowers attributes like courage, compassion, a calm demeanor, problem-solving skills, the ability to take risks, resilience to make an impact in the business environment, and the ability to survive the ever-changing role of the assistant.

This is a book not only for the assistant but all business leaders. When a business leader takes time to understand the strengths of an assistant, it frees them to be more strategic and productive. Hopefully, assistants and leaders will relate to the stories in this book and use the key takeaways to improve their skills, knowledge, and understanding of the role.

The administrative profession has changed over the past few decades. Assistants used to be task-doers. Their role has evolved to more of a business partner, handling responsibilities beyond answering the phone, typing correspondence, and managing expense reports. They are now more engaged in the aspects of the business. They have influence, provide insight, make suggestions to improve processes, and help the executive focus on major business results. With technology and skill, assistants seek ways to be efficient and effective business partners. They are more empowered than in the past, and many have an amazing impact on the day-to-day business decisions.

If you enjoyed these stories, please share some of your own by emailing me at my business (linda@ascend2success.com) or my personal email (ceo1shadow@gmail.com). Enjoy!

A dream doesn't become reality
through magic; it takes sweat,
determination and hard work.

—COLIN POWELL

Wizards Bend Things to Their Will

MAY I SERVE YOU?

Here is a story about a normal board meeting event. It all started with a few ad hoc meetings scheduled during the lunch hour. If only someone had mentioned that the restaurant had made some changes during a downturn in the economy!

I was driving through traffic during commute time to our offsite board meeting, which was scheduled to take place at a hotel in the quaint town of Los Gatos, California. Traffic was light, so I was taking in the scenic beauty—something I rarely take the time to do. As I drove, I kept going through the meeting details in my head to make sure that I had dotted all my i's and crossed all my t's.

One thing on my list had been a request by our CEO to schedule a premeeting with some of our board members and staff. Having had many previous meetings at this hotel, I suggested they meet over lunch in the hotel restaurant. This seemed like the perfect solution for a productive meeting.

THE WIZARD BEHIND THE CEO

Plus, they wouldn't have to spend an extra hour in a conference room, especially since the room where they would be holding their meeting didn't have any natural light. The CEO liked this idea, so I had reserved space at the restaurant.

I arrived at the hotel with plenty of time to check the conference room setup and review all the details one last time with my hotel contact. She handled all the onsite meeting details for the hotel. We chatted briefly about a few adjustments to the logistics, some catering changes during the meeting, and timing for the arrival of the board members and other attendees.

I made my way to the lobby to greet the guests and direct them to the restaurant across the hall, as the lunch meeting would be starting in less than 15 minutes.

As I was waiting, the restaurant hostess and I spoke for a moment. We had met previously during an onsite meeting, and our conversation wasn't unusual. During our chat, I mentioned that our team would be meeting over lunch in the restaurant at noon.

"I'll be departing around noon," the hostess casually mentioned.

At first, I thought she was sharing some details about her day and replied, "Have a nice afternoon."

Thank heaven she followed up with another question: "Will your group need food for their meeting, or will they just use the restaurant space?"

I thought, "How nice of her to be so interested in my meeting!" and then politely said, "Yes, I thought it would make more sense to have lunch here instead of taking extra time to walk to a nearby restaurant. That way, they will be steps away from the conference room where their next meeting will be held."

"Did you place a special catering order for your group?"

"No," I responded. "I thought they could just order off the menu and charge it to our master bill like we've done in the past." Then I thought, "Why is she asking about the details? Maybe she is just being polite since she will soon be departing."

Her next question finally made me think more clearly: "You do realize that the restaurant is closed during the lunch hour, right?"

It took me a few seconds to process what she was telling me; in fact, I still wasn't getting it.

"What do you mean?"

"I'll be leaving at noon because our restaurant closes at that time, and we don't open again until 5:00 p.m. when we serve dinner," she patiently replied.

All at once, her questions made complete sense.

No one had informed me about that restaurant change since my last visit just a few months earlier. The restaurant had always been open during the lunch hour, so I hadn't thought to check on that detail.

Seeing my deer-in-the-headlights stare, she continued. "If you haven't made arrangements with our catering department, your group won't get any lunch. Our servers won't return until we reopen at 5:00 p.m., and we have a limited kitchen crew between now and 5:00 p.m."

I could sense that she was getting tired of repeating the same message. Perhaps if she had been more direct, the message would have resonated sooner—or perhaps if I had listened to what she was saying, I would have figured it out already.

She continued to maintain her professional demeanor with a smile on her face. That's when it finally sunk in. I had a place for our meeting, but there just wouldn't be any food for them to eat!

"No service during the lunch hour?" I asked in a panicked voice. "When did this change?"

She calmly explained that about a month ago the hotel had done some cost cutting. This took place during a downturn in the economy, and every company, including hotels, was looking for ways to trim costs. The restaurant didn't generate enough business during lunch, so hotel management had decided to close the restaurant during that time—at least for the next several months.

I could hear my heart pounding in my ears. My thoughts quickly went to my list of nearby restaurants: pizza, salads, soup, or maybe sushi? I pictured a pizza delivery truck arriving with a stack of pizza boxes for our executive meeting. That just wasn't going to work. I headed to the front desk in search of my hotel contact. Perhaps between the two of us, we could come up with another plan.

She appeared within a few minutes, and I gave her a rundown of my dilemma.

"I'm concerned about getting food for my group. I have never been a waitress before, but if you can get your chef to make some food, I'll serve it."

She gave me a reassuring look and raised her index finger in the air.

"I have an idea. Now I just need a buy-in from the chef. Give me just a minute. Let me see what I can do," she said as she disappeared into the kitchen.

Those few minutes seemed like an hour. The meeting attendees had arrived at the restaurant and were already seated. They had no idea of the drama inside my head or what was taking place in the kitchen. I thought it was best to simply get them seated, so I walked them to their table and told them their server would be with them shortly.

To my relief, the hotel contact soon reappeared from the kitchen.

"All my guests have arrived," I told her with angst in my voice. Before she could get a word out, I added, "What's the plan? Remember, I can be a server if that's what it will take."

She smiled, nodded her head, headed for the hostess area, and grabbed a dozen menus.

"Okay," she began. "I talked to the chef and explained the situation..It took some pleading, but he agreed to provide some lunch items for your group. However, you'll have to tell them they can only order from the left side of the menu as the other options aren't available. Are you sure you want to be the server?" she asked with an apprehensive look.

"There's always a first time for everything," I replied.

I located my small notebook and pen, grabbed the menus, and off I went with the hotel contact not far behind for some much-needed moral support.

As I approached the CEO's chair, he greeted me with a smile and then leaned toward me, assuming I was delivering a message or giving him an update on a board-related matter.

"Hello everyone," I said. "I have some good news, and I have some bad news. First, the bad news: As of a month ago, the restaurant no longer serves lunch. The good news is that the chef has agreed to a limited menu. Now, for more good news: My name is Linda, and I'll be your server. Today is my first day on the job."

They all laughed.

The CEO handled the situation with ease and added, "Of course we're delighted that you will be our server." Then he turned to the board members and staff and said, "Linda is the best assistant I've ever had. She can figure out how to get anything done. Shall we place our order?"

With that, they all smiled, made a few humorous comments, placed their orders, and off I went to deliver the selections to the chef.

The real entertainment began when I went to fill their beverage orders. No one was behind the bar, and I had no idea where to begin. My hotel contact was nearby and immediately came to my rescue, although both of us were very much out of our element. We pushed a few buttons and laughed hysterically as we tried to fill the soda requests. Working together, we figured it out and served the drinks and meals with finesse (at least, as far as they knew). All the attendees commented that the food was great and the service was impeccable. I blushed a little with embarrassment, but I pulled it off.

After getting everyone off to the next meeting, I profusely thanked the kitchen staff for coming to my rescue in the eleventh hour and for teaching me some new skills, which I contemplated adding to my resume. The hotel contact was such a good sport, and the situation bound us as friends for life.

WAND
(What Assistants Need Daily)

✳ Like wizards, when you get in situations outside of your realm of experience, remain open-minded, take a chance, and learn new skills.

* If you're planning an offsite meeting, double-check all details, even if you think nothing has changed.

* It takes more skill to listen than to hear a message, so be sure to take time to listen to those communicating with you.

* Use clarifying phrases like "Tell me more" or "Help me understand" when you question someone's understanding of your intended message. You can also use "who, what, where, when, and why" questions.

* If you have a "can-do" attitude, small glitches in a plan can be resolved with minimal stress and a lot of ingenuity.

* When details don't come together, check all your options (even improbable ones).

* When you work with a team committed to a good outcome, it's more fun than doing everything yourself.

* If you need to make special arrangements, don't be afraid to ask for help. If you explain the situation, exceptions can be made.

* Instead of putting blame on others, work together to find an amicable solution.

The greatest discovery of my
generation is that a human being can
alter his life by altering his attitude.

—WILLIAM JAMES

Wizards Are Held in High Standing

FIRST-CLASS TREATMENT

An upcoming organizational announcement requires discretion with strict confidentiality and puts values to the test. Will choices lead to trustworthiness and a lasting business partnership with the CEO?

I traveled with my CEO to special customer and partner events and conferences. One Las Vegas conference was grueling, and we worked 14- to 16-hour days. It was the last day of the event, and we were scheduled to travel back to San Jose the next day.

I approached the CEO to review some semiurgent pending items. He was exhausted from the intense week and suggested we review the items during our flight home.

"Reviewing the items on the plane sounds great," I responded with slight sarcasm in my voice. "The only hitch is that I am traveling coach, and you've been upgraded to first class."

That made him smile. The next words out of his mouth really surprised me.

"Linda, go ahead and use my miles to upgrade your flight to first class. Make sure we're seated together. That way we can cover all the pending items before we land."

"Did I get that right?" I thought. "Did he just tell me that I'd be traveling in FIRST CLASS?"

In the three-plus years I worked with this executive, I seldom had the luxury to travel in first class. In fact, I had never flown first class—ever! I was feeling very special. Though Las Vegas to San Jose was a short flight, first-class travel is, well, *first-class travel.*

The look on my face was enough for him to know that I was pleased.

"You deserve it, Linda! You should plan to take the car service with me to the airport too. Anything else?"

"Nope. And thank you!"

I rushed to upgrade my ticket before he changed his mind. I relished the idea of comfort in a limo and first-class treatment. Lucky me!

The next morning, traffic was clear. We made it to the airport with time to spare.

Since we had extra time, my boss said, "Linda, let's go to the Red Carpet Club and get some snacks before the flight."

Wow, the Red Carpet Club! My boss spent lots of time in and out of the Red Carpet Club. My only relevant experience was making sure the annual fee was paid and knowing which airports had a Red Carpet Club or Lounge. I was finally going to have the pleasure of enjoying the amenities and relaxing environment instead of an uncomfortable seat in the gate area (if one were even available).

It felt good to have this first-class treatment after such a busy week. My feet were feeling the pain from the many laps through the hotel to ensure smooth-running meetings.

Once we were comfortably seated in the Red Carpet Club, I took a deep breath, glanced out the window at the air traffic, and smiled. After a slow, quenching beverage, it was time to get to business and review the action list with my boss.

"Linda, there's no rush to review the list. I have some things you and I need to discuss. Some very confidential items, and I'm going to need your help. In fact, the only people who know about this are a few board members, myself, and now you."

I promptly ceased sipping my beverage and fixed my attention; this wasn't the time to miss anything. My boss began to tell me about his decision to move from CEO to executive chairman. He would be promoting our chief operating officer (COO) to the CEO position. Our COO had been doing a great job, and my boss felt that it was the perfect time to make the change. It would take a few months to get all the details aligned, and he needed my help to put together the transition plan among other things. He made it clear that it needed to be done with the utmost discretion as the COO was not yet aware of this organizational change.

I must admit that he surprised me. This meant that our almost four-year assistant/executive partnership would be coming to an end. This CEO was truly a great leader—someone who had tremendous respect from the employees and the business community. During the past four-plus years, the CEO had enhanced the culture of the company, hired an excellent leadership team, increased revenues, and led with integrity. I shook off the shock of the news and put aside my personal fears and concerns. I was grateful that he trusted me enough to share the news about the organizational change.

We worked together and soon the announcement day arrived. I'll never forget when the CEO gave a departing speech during the event where many of our employees were gathered. I looked around the room, and there was hardly a dry eye in the place. What a beloved CEO! Although we had faith in our new leader, we were grateful for all that the outgoing CEO had done to make our company great again and an amazing place to work. Not only was he a humble leader, he was a great teacher and mentor—even if he didn't recognize it at the time.

As I reflected on my excitement about getting an upgrade to first class and a limo ride to the airport, I realized that there was much more I had learned that day. My boss had entrusted me with a highly confidential matter. He showed me that he had confidence in my ability to be trustworthy and credible and considered me as someone with high integrity. I will always be grateful for that gift and the lessons he taught me.

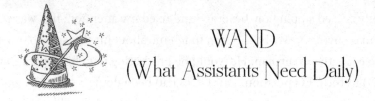

WAND
(What Assistants Need Daily)

✳ Be true to your values and be trustworthy, like the behavior of wizards. An executive's trust is the highest compliment.

✳ Use extreme discretion when receiving confidential information.

✳ Establish credibility by standing by your values, keeping commitments, listening to others, and continually learning new things.

✳ Be familiar with your executive's goals, seek to understand their work style, and establish checkpoints to stay aligned.

Those who trust us, educate us.

—GEORGE ELIOT, *DANIEL DERONDA*

Wizards Have Magical Powers

COMMUNICATION MIX-UP

In this story, a communication mix-up with a vendor causes immense stress. Keeping calm and building relationships help secure a new reliable vendor for life!

It was that time again. Each quarter, our executive team traveled to offices outside the United States for a week of back-to-back meetings. On occasion, when our CEO visited other company locations, he would hold a face-to-face, all-hands company meeting with the employees located in that office. At least a few times a year, we would organize one of these meetings during our visit.

While setting up the week's schedule, I asked our CEO about adding the all-hands company meeting during this trip as we had done in the past. It had only been a few months since our last visit, so he decided that we didn't need to schedule one. I made a note and finished arrangements for the other meetings. To make things efficient for the executives, I organized ground transportation, a hotel room block, product reviews, and additional meetings as requested.

Before I knew it, the date had arrived. During this trip, I was having some issues with our new ground-transportation vendor. Although I caught the mistakes in time, some of the confirmation details for the return flights were still wrong. Since I didn't have the confidence and trust with the vendor, I kept a keen eye on the project. That meant reconfirming the details for each executive's ground transportation 24 hours before departure. While I didn't welcome the extra task, the last thing I needed was one of our executives stranded because his arranged transportation didn't show.

I created a detailed spreadsheet that included everyone's travel information and the name and mobile number of the assigned drivers. Having this information at my fingertips helped give me peace of mind that these arrangements would go smoothly. Now, if only I could get the vendor to keep things straight!

A few days into our weeklong schedule, our CEO approached me.

"Hi, Linda. I'd like to add an all-hands company meeting to the schedule for the office. Let's hold it in the afternoon before we depart for the airport tomorrow."

"You got it," I replied with assurance. "If only he had let me add this meeting when we first talked," I thought. "Everything would already be in place."

I let that thought go and got busy. I reviewed the schedule for Thursday afternoon. The only time available was between 3:30 and 4:30 pm. That would just have to do.

Next, I knew that I had to bring the facility's coordinator and receptionist up to speed. They would have a short turnaround for organizing logistics, catering needs, and the meeting invite. Thank heaven the onsite team was easy to work with and responsive. All the details came together, and the meeting was planned.

With the addition of the all-hands company meeting, I decided that it would be best to have our CEO travel to the airport in a separate car. He was originally scheduled to share a car with a few staff members, including me. Holding the all-hands company meeting in the afternoon meant a later departure from the office to the airport for everyone. None of us had a global entry card, so making our way through the airport required more time, especially for those who needed to check their luggage.

While the CEO wrapped up the meeting, the rest of us headed for the airport. Although the weather was stormy, we made it with time to spare. I let my guard down a little as every driver was where they were supposed to be at their designated time. No setbacks yet today. I had reconfirmed the CEO's pickup time and details earlier in the day, so I wasn't worried about his transportation.

After checking in and making our way through the airport, we looked for a place to eat before our flights departed. I looked down at my phone to check the time and saw four missed calls from our CEO.

"Yikes!" I said in a panic to those traveling with me. "Something must be wrong. My boss has called me four times!"

I quickly called him back and asked, "Is everything okay?"

"No, I'm *not* okay," he responded with a sense of panic. "I'm in the lobby at the office, and I don't see any driver. Did you forget about me?"

I swallowed hard before I answered: "Let me call the driver, and I'll call you right back."

By this time, we were seated in the airport restaurant. The other executive with me could hear one side of the conversation and became curious.

I hung up the phone and nervously pulled out my sheet with the travel details and drivers' numbers.

I looked at the other executive and said, "His driver didn't show, so I need to make a quick call."

Although I appeared very calm to the other executive, I wasn't. The last thing I needed was for my boss to miss his flight. I felt like a duck on water: calmly gliding on the top of the water but paddling like crazy underneath!

I dialed the driver's number and was relieved when he picked up the phone. I asked if he was already onsite to pick up my boss. His response made the hair on the back of my neck stand straight up and scream, if that were possible.

"No, I'm not. Your vendor called me earlier today and told me that no car service was needed for your CEO. He didn't provide any further explanation. I thought it was strange but figured his plans must have changed."

I let out a gasp. Just when I thought everything was going well, there was another wrinkle in the plan.

"Are you available right now?"

"I'm just dropping off another client at the airport. Shall I go get him now?"

My heart sank. Our office was more than 20 minutes away from the airport. If the driver headed back to get him now, he wouldn't arrive in time to catch his flight—even with global entry access.

"I don't think he'll make it in time," I informed him with a tone of disappointment. "He needs to depart in the next five to 10 minutes in order to make his flight."

"Let me make a call. I may have a driver in the area." He must have sensed my desperation, and I was so grateful that he was willing to help.

"THANK YOU! I don't know how I can ever repay you for being so generous and kind and especially taking your precious time to help me fix this."

I hung up the phone and said a silent prayer: "Please, God. I need a little miracle."

A quick text let my boss know that I would have an update in a few minutes. I could tell by his reply that he was getting anxious and for good reason. If he missed this flight, he'd have to wait until morning to catch the next flight home.

By this time, the executive with me was even more curious about what had transpired. With a genuinely caring tone in her voice, she said, "You are the calmest person I've ever met! It's been fun watching you in action."

Little did she know that, although I was calm on the outside, I was still quite stressed on the inside.

She continued, "Are you going to tell our boss the recent series of events?"

"Let's keep that between us for now," I suggested. "I hope the driver will call back with a doable plan. If not, I'll need to get a taxi right away."

Seconds later, my phone rang. It was the driver with good news!

"I have a car five minutes from your executive's location," he explained. "He's on the way there now. We can sort payment details later." He gave further instructions about where to meet the driver.

Now to call my boss.

"Hi again. Your driver will be there in five minutes. Meet him across the street in front of the hotel. You should arrive on time as traffic seems light today."

"Great! I'll head there now."

I glanced at the executive with me and said, "Fingers crossed that he makes it."

As soon as we finished dinner, my boss was standing at our table in the restaurant. He made it in record time.

"Oh, *fine*," he said humorously. "Have dinner while I'm stuck in the rain, trying to find my car. That's the *last* time I'll let you take a car ahead of me!" He laughed, and then sat down to join us for a quick dinner.

Phew! He made it, and he still had a sense of humor. We all made our flights, and I had gained a new friend that day and a new vendor.

A few weeks later, I shared the real story with our CEO. We had a good laugh about it. He teased me for weeks and poked fun about how I could never depart before him again from any event. It was a much more enjoyable experience sharing the story *after* the fact. When you must deliver bad news, timing is everything!

WAND
(What Assistants Need Daily)

❋ Keep calm. It's easier to think when you don't let the situation get the best of you.

❋ Be professional and kind. Losing your temper will only create unneeded drama.

* Keep your composure to help you think more clearly and build long-lasting relationships.

* Whenever possible, check the ratings and testimonials of new vendors.

* Check in with your network to see if someone has vendor recommendations for locations unfamiliar to you.

* When you're in transit and your boss is traveling too, be diligent about checking your email and text messages, and keep in touch with your boss to avoid miscommunication or confusion.

* Provide feedback to the vendor to let them know when things have gone wrong. It's the only way they will improve in the future.

* Keep critical numbers in your contact list. Be sure to have local taxi numbers available too.

One learns in life to keep silent and
draw one's own confusions.

—CORNELIA OTIS SKINNER

Wizards Have the Power of Observation

THE GOOSE COACH

This story shows how compassion during a difficult time brings out unknown talents from the administrative team and a bond that will stand the test of time.

Did you know that each goose flaps its wings to create uplift for birds that follow? They share a common direction and a sense of community. When a goose falls out of formation, it feels the drag of resistance of flying alone and quickly moves back into formation. To me, this behavior shows their willingness to accept help and give help to others. The lead goose knows how to share leadership too. When it tires, it rotates back into the formation and another goose takes the point position. What a great way to take turns doing hard tasks!

Do you ever wonder why geese honk so much when they fly? It encourages the geese in the front of the formation to keep going. That fact has taught me to be more encouraging to coworkers and avoid gossip and backbiting.

When a goose gets sick, two geese drop out of formation and follow it down to help protect it until it can fly again—or, sadly, until it dies. Then the geese look for another formation to join or they catch up with the original flock.

Geese truly know how to stand by each other in difficult and good times. This fact resonates with me, and here's why:

I was tasked with putting together a last-minute offsite meeting for 80 people. I had about three weeks to pull all the details together, and I was feeling a little frantic. Hotel contracts, travel arrangements, ground transportation, onsite details, communication emails, and so much more.

I had just signed the final hotel contract to secure the venue. This was only the beginning of a very long task list, and time was running out.

As I pulled the checklist together, I received a call from my husband that his father had less than 24 hours to live. I had to leave and would probably be unavailable for a few days. How was I going to pull the details together now? I was feeling overwhelmed and anxious.

My CEO was in a meeting, so I sent him a text about the circumstances. Within a few minutes, my phone rang. It was the assistant for our marketing department. She had already heard about my father-in-law.

"Linda, I heard the sad news. I know you are working on this big event. I'd like to help."

I knew that this assistant had a heavy workload.

"Are you sure?"

"Of course," she said. "I can help organize the travel arrangements for the attendees or anything else."

She was at my desk in record time. We reviewed the attendee list along with some ideas for the dinner events. She assured me that she would get the travel details together and research dinner venues. I was feeling much better about the situation, so off I went to pay my last respects.

My father-in-law died hours later. I attended his funeral and, a few days later, I was back to work. The marketing assistant had done an amazing job pulling the attendees' travel details together. She gave me a quick overview of what had been done during my absence.

As we reviewed the outstanding items, she shared that she enjoyed event planning and couldn't wait to participate. We quickly divided and conquered the other tasks. Assignments were made to determine who would communicate details, prepare spreadsheets, and contact vendors.

Our personalities meshed, and the details of the event were coming together with ease. In the final few days before the event, we discussed the registration process for the participants' arrival. It became evident that we both needed to be at the hotel on Saturday evening to make sure that everything was in place for the attendees' arrival on Sunday afternoon. There was one small problem: The shuttles for the attendees were scheduled to depart from the corporate office on Sunday. Who could we get to handle this little snag?

One of the other assistants stopped by my desk. She heard that we were working on some last-minute items and wondered if we needed any help. *Perfect timing!* I told her about our situation and the need to have someone at the corporate office on Sunday to get everyone on the shuttles. Would she be willing to give up her Sunday?

"No problem!" she said. "I can be here."

What a relief to know that she was willing to give up her precious Sunday afternoon to help us. We briefed her on all the details and felt confident about the plan.

As my boss passed by my desk, I gave him a quick update. Then, he surprised me with a new task. He and a few of the executives were avid cyclists. Since the weather was good that time of year, they decided to cycle to the venue together.

"Seriously?" I asked. "That's a really long ride. What about your luggage? How will you get your bikes home?"

He smiled like the Cheshire Cat to indicate that it was an easy request, or perhaps he knew it wasn't his concern.

"Linda, you're a seasoned assistant. I know you will figure it out." With that, he stepped into his office for the next meeting.

My mind immediately went to problem-solving mode. We had enough seats in the shuttles, but where would we put the extra bikes on the return home? I connected with the two assistants who were helping organize the event. After a brief brainstorming session, we came up with a plan.

Problem solved. For the return, we added a small shuttle to transport the luggage and bikes.

The day of the event arrived. As planned, the marketing assistant and I headed to the hotel on Saturday night. The next morning, we set up the registration desk and put together all the goodies for the swag bag that was to be given to each attendee.

While we were busy at the hotel, attendees started arriving at the office from all parts of the world to board the shuttles. We kept in touch with the assistant at the office using our mobile phones. She made sure that the extra luggage for the cyclists was loaded.

My phone rang, and I could see it was the assistant. I answered, hoping to hear that all was well and that the shuttle was on the way.

"Hi! How is it going?"

"Almost everyone has arrived. I need some direction. One flight is delayed with three attendees. Shall I send the shuttle without them? People are ready to depart, and some have been here a long time. They're getting antsy."

"Yes, let's get everyone on the way. I'll text those on the flight. We'll make other arrangements for them."

"Great!" she said with a sigh of relief. After a pause, she continued. "There's one more thing. Someone here is claiming to be an attendee, but he's not on my list. What do I do?"

"Oh, my!" I said with surprise. "Who is it?"

We quickly got things sorted. Apparently, there had been a discussion with the CEO and one of his staff members about a last-minute addition. Sadly, they forgot to tell me. Those are the days when I wish I was telepathic.

The marketing assistant and I were on it. We arranged a hotel room for him, added him to the list of attendees, and the shuttles departed. Thank goodness we had an assistant at the office to manage the logistics and the people.

Soon everyone arrived at the hotel—even the cyclists. The offsite meeting took place, and even the small glitches weren't noticed because of our collaborative efforts. We all agreed that, although there was so much work involved, we learned about each other and our skills—and even had fun! The gestures of compassion shown to me during this difficult time bonded our team for years to come.

WAND
(What Assistants Need Daily)

✳ Like wizards, form groups or councils with other assistants to strengthen your knowledge.

✳ Try to get to know your coworkers. We all have many distinctive skills and talents.

✳ Asking your coworkers for input and feedback will create synergy and new learning opportunities.

✳ Don't compare yourself to others. We are each unique and have much to offer.

✳ Be nice. Be genuine.

✳ Be compassionate with your team members. You never know when you might need support.

✳ To build relationships, share something about you to create a connection.

✳ Figure out each other's strengths. Divide and conquer.

✳ Share best practices with your colleagues.

✳ Ask yourself what you have to offer your team and what support you need from them.

✳ Resist the impulse to become offended when someone doesn't handle something the way you might have hoped.

✳ Evaluate the lessons we can learn from geese and their collaborative nature:

    ✳ Share a common direction and a sense of community.

    ✳ Be willing to accept help and give help to others.

    ✳ Take turns doing hard tasks.

    ✳ Share leadership opportunities.

    ✳ Make sure your honking is encouraging.

    ✳ Stand by each other in difficult and good times.

It is amazing how much people can get done if they do not worry about who gets the credit.

—SANDRA SWINNEY

Wizards Recover Quickly

ADVENTURES IN GERMANY

Organizing last-minute offsite meetings in a foreign country comes with a unique set of challenges, especially when you don't speak the language.

Have you ever had to organize an event in a foreign country where English wasn't the spoken language? I've planned hundreds of events, and most of them have taken place in the United States or in English-speaking countries.

I was working on the quarterly offsite meeting agenda for our leadership team, which was scheduled to take place outside of London. About five weeks before the event, our CEO decided to change the venue to our office in Germany. One of our assistants, who was in that office, volunteered to help facilitate the logistics and be the onsite support for the team. I was relieved to know that I wouldn't need to travel and was happy to let the Germany assistant take the lead.

We had a few phone conversations to talk about the details, and the priority was to secure hotel rooms. We needed 30+ rooms, and our CEO was hoping for a room-block contract with the hotel located steps away from the office. It was a popular hotel and, with such short notice, reserving 30+ rooms would be a stretch. To our disappointment, the hotel was sold out.

The Germany assistant offered to make calls to nearby hotels. That made it much easier since she was in the same time zone. She had some luck finding a location that could accommodate our group. The only drawback was that it was located 15-20 minutes from the Germany office. She assured me that they had a reliable transportation company, which could provide daily transportation to and from the office.

"I'll make all the arrangements," she said, reassuring me that she was very capable of handling the details.

I got busy working with the CEO on the list of attendees and the agenda.

"Linda, one more thing," the CEO said. "Let's plan to hold our quarterly all-hands company meeting at the Germany office following the offsite meeting. Be sure to have the film crew available so we can broadcast to all the offices and record it for those not in the same time zone."

I knew this request would require lots of planning and organizing. I would handle all those details and have the other assistant support them when they arrived onsite in Germany. I sent an email to give the assistant a heads-up about the meeting and to figure out the logistics and other details.

The agenda was now complete, and our CEO sent it to the attendees. I emailed the logistics to them and gathered their travel details. Since the Germany assistant was the lead to set up the hotel reservations and ground transportation, I sent her the arrival and departure dates for each attendee. I then asked that she forward the confirmation numbers so that I could communicate the details to everyone. I knew it was in good hands now.

A week passed, and it was now less than three weeks from the event date. I still hadn't heard back from the assistant, so I sent a follow-up email. A few more days went by with no reply. It wasn't like her not to respond. I called her number, and it went straight to voicemail, so I left a message. Another day went by and still no response. I decided to contact the receptionist. Maybe she would know how to reach the assistant.

When she picked up the phone, I asked if the assistant was in the office.

Imagine my surprise when she responded, "She went on medical leave a few weeks ago. We're not sure about her return date. She may be out for a few months."

"*Medical leave*?" I repeated.

Suddenly I felt short of breath. I completely understand when people need to take medical leave. What I didn't comprehend is why no one told me. I tried to compose myself. Since there were no other assistants in our Germany office, the only thought in my head was "Now what?" I knew that I needed a backup plan before talking with the CEO. All these thoughts raced through my mind. The receptionist didn't speak very good English, which made me nervous.

"Let me have you talk with the other receptionist," she said in her broken English. "She speaks and understands English much better than I do."

I composed myself and spoke with the other receptionist. Although she spoke English well, I realized that many details were getting lost in translation. This was going to be more challenging than I had anticipated.

I was still a bit overwhelmed with the news. There was no way I could expect the receptionist to organize this large and very important offsite meeting. I had Plan B, but it meant that I would need to travel to Germany.

I apprised the CEO of the new situation. He agreed that it made sense for me to make the trip, provide support, and assist with the logistics. Now the fun part: setting up the catering, hotel rooms, all-hands logistics, and transportation details in advance of my arrival with the event only a few weeks away.

Setting up the room block with the hotel was easy. The assistant on leave had already finalized the hotel contract. The only thing left to do was set up the rooming list. I could handle that with ease.

I found a reliable transportation company that handled the rides from the airport to the hotel, with a drive time of about 1-1/2 hours. For the daily rides to and from the hotel to the office, the receptionist volunteered to set up a shuttle with a local transportation company. I could check this task off my list.

Catering was a different story. I had several email exchanges with the receptionist about the food, including dietary restrictions. I was adamant that we needed specific arrangements for each day, especially with the various dietary needs of the attendees. As we exchanged emails, it was clear again that items were being lost in translation. I was worried about the lack of understanding and tried to figure out how I was going to get the details properly communicated.

I remembered that one of our executives grew up there and spoke German. She agreed to help translate the catering details. We set up a conference call with the receptionist, and I listened in (not that it did any good since I didn't understand a word they said!).

After lots of extra communication with all the vendors and our receptionist, it finally felt like the details were coming together. Now it was time to make my way to Germany.

When I met the driver upon arrival, I was thankful that he spoke English. It was a Sunday afternoon, and the offsite meeting didn't begin until Tuesday. I planned to double-check all the arrangements on Monday, including the conference room. I alerted the information technology (IT) staff that I would also need support for the meeting and arranged to meet them on Monday as well.

While checking in at the hotel, I found that the front desk staff spoke very little English, but I didn't let that change my positive attitude. With some kind words and a gentle smile, I was checked in.

I opened the door to my hotel room to find two very small twin-sized beds. I'm almost 6' tall. If I wasn't going to fit in the bed, how would the other attendees manage? I pushed the two beds together to give me more room and curled up with my knees bent to take a short nap. It was going to be a long week in a short bed.

After my brief nap, I took a stroll around the hotel. We were scheduled to hold a dinner onsite Tuesday night. I easily located the conference room I had scheduled as it was a small hotel. I continued down the hallway and found the fitness center.

"Hmmm …" I thought. "Maybe I'll do a quick workout."

I walked in and realized that the area was very small and hot. I had no interest in spending any time in that area. I grabbed the doorknob of what I thought was the exit. To my surprise, a loud alarm went off. You would have thought I was robbing the place! I quickly made my way back to the door I had entered, hoping no one would notice that I caused all the noise. It was so embarrassing! I found my way back to my room, ate a protein bar, and watched German TV. I was still feeling the effects of a new time zone and jet lag, so getting back to sleep was easy.

The next morning, I was up early. I wanted to get to the office to find my way around and meet the IT staff and receptionists. My cab driver didn't speak English, so I showed him the address for the office. He looked up at me and at the address again. He stepped out of the cab, found someone to translate it for him, and off we went. Luck was with me, and the cab pulled up to our office. I found my way to the lobby. *I made it!* I introduced myself to the receptionists and got settled at a desk where I'd work for the rest of the week.

I was anxious to see the conference room where the meetings would take place, so I poked my head into the room. *Ugh!* The setup was all wrong. I tracked down the facilities person, introduced myself, and suggested some changes to get the room set up just right. I was happy with the new layout, although it was obvious that it would be a tight fit for the number of attendees.

Next, I made my way to the IT staff room where I was introduced to my onsite tech-support person. We talked about what the CEO required for the meeting. I stressed the importance of having everything ready on time, so the meeting could start as planned. A laptop would be required for the presentations. He mentioned that it would take several hours to get the laptop ready, and off he went, determined to meet the deadline.

After several hours of work, I was soon back at the hotel. I was still feeling a little jet lag and went right to bed.

The next morning, we were scheduled for breakfast in the restaurant before departing for the office. I went downstairs early to check out the food. The hotel had a large staff, and breakfast was delicious. As I finished, I saw other attendees enjoying the food and visiting with each other. So far, no one had complained about the rooms and especially the size of the beds. Maybe my room was the exception.

I walked to the lobby, hoping to see our shuttle bus outside. I was sure the driver would arrive early, but no shuttle. I went back and forth outside for at least 10-15 minutes. Now it was 10 minutes before we were scheduled to depart.

I called the transportation company every five minutes and kept getting an answering machine. The message was in German, but that didn't stop me from leaving messages. Another five minutes went by and still no call back. I searched for the executive who spoke German. Thank heaven she was among the attendees. We dialed again and still got the answering machine. She left a message in German. By now, attendees began to gather outside the hotel to board the shuttle.

I turned to look at the 30 attendees standing in the cold. My boss pushed his way through the crowd.

"What's going on? Where's the shuttle?" he demanded with intense authority.

It was my third month on the job, and the last thing I wanted to say was, "I don't know!"

I hesitated and finally replied, "I'm not sure. I've been calling my contact at the ground transportation company, and I keep getting an answering machine. I don't have anyone's mobile number either."

Before I could say another word, the CEO cut me off. "Well, how do you expect us to get to the office? Now we are running late!"

I was at a loss for words.

Before I could say anything, my boss commanded, "Let's call for taxis!" He turned away and quickly headed for the hotel lobby.

It made me feel completely incompetent and helpless. The crowd parted like the Red Sea as the CEO walked by.

They all looked at me as if to say, "Boy, we sure don't want to be *you* right now."

I apologized that the shuttle had not arrived and told them that we were going to get some taxis to take us to the office.

I joined the CEO at the front desk where he was already giving commands. The entire staff was on high alert. One of the clerks was ordering several taxis while another was handing my boss euros.

"Charge it to my room," he said in a harried voice.

He glanced up at me with what I felt was pure disgust and, without saying a word, he brushed by me and headed outside. The taxis had begun arriving and, even before we made our way outside the lobby, attendees were piling in the cars and bolting. No one wanted to be around for the wrath of the CEO.

He looked at his watch and said, "Now we'll be about 10 minutes behind on our start time."

It was the first offsite meeting I had planned since my arrival. It certainly didn't feel like I was making a great first impression. I'd have to make up for it later.

I jumped in a cab with some of the attendees. They tried to make light of the situation. I smiled but kept silent. Where was the shuttle? Why didn't I get a call back? I'd have to get to the bottom of this as soon as possible. I couldn't fathom the thought of a repeat incident for the ride back to the hotel.

As soon as we arrived at the office, I sprinted to the conference room. I wanted to make sure the laptop was ready to go. As I stepped into the room, I looked around. No laptop. My heart raced. No shuttle and now no laptop? I ran to the IT area to find my contact. I was relieved and somewhat irritated to see him sitting at his desk.

"I don't see the laptop in the conference room. Is there a problem?" I quickly asked.

I was trying to keep calm, but I was really frustrated. We had been over the details. I thought I had been very clear that the laptop needed to be set up and ready to go by 8:00 AM.

"I can set it up now. No worries," he responded with a lackadaisical attitude as he headed out the door to the conference room.

My jaw dropped, and my mouth was open. "Really?" I thought. I responded with a somewhat audacious tone and said, "We're already 10 minutes late. Since we must take time to set up, it's going to push the agenda to an even later time."

Before I could ask any more questions, he was out the door. He must have sensed my anxiety and quickly picked up his pace.

As we entered the room, most of the team was already seated at the table. He opened the laptop, and I couldn't believe my eyes: Everything was in German. *This was a disaster!* I hadn't even thought about the laptop being in a different language. I just didn't have enough experience with how things operated at companies in foreign countries. Boy, was I naïve. Plus, the IT guy didn't even mention that to me! He did his best to swiftly set up the laptop and launched into a quick tutorial for my boss on how it worked.

The CEO looked at the laptop, then at the IT guy, and then at me. Before the IT guy could give any further instructions, the CEO unplugged and closed the laptop with exasperation. With a hard push, it flew to the end of the table.

"We've wasted enough time on this," he said with no apology. He announced that each presenter would need to use their own laptop for their presentation and quickly dismissed me and the IT guy. "You can take that laptop with you as we won't need it."

The IT guy just stood there frozen. I gave him a gentle nudge toward the door and closed it behind us.

"I was only trying to help," he said with disbelief. He was rattled.

With a calm, professional voice, I said, "He likes his meetings to run on time. Not having the laptop set up put them behind. We were already running late since the shuttle didn't show up this morning. I know you spent a lot of time getting the laptop ready, but it appears that we won't be using it after all. This one is on me. Please don't worry."

He slowly walked back to the IT area with the laptop. His first encounter with the CEO wasn't very pleasant. Luckily, he would have a chance to turn things around during our all-hands company meeting.

Before walking back to my work area, I stopped in the lobby to check in with the receptionist about the ground transportation.

"Our shuttle didn't show up this morning. Did you get a message from them yesterday or today? We ended up organizing some taxis to get everyone to the office. It completely threw off the schedule and caused the meeting to get a late start. Boy, was my boss unhappy."

"What? It didn't show? We didn't hear anything," the receptionist said.

"Could you please call to find out what happened? I'd really appreciate your help on this one, especially since I don't speak the language. Let's reach out to the company that provided transportation from the airport. They were very reliable. Perhaps they could provide a shuttle for the rest of the week. We definitely won't be using the other vendor."

"I can do that for you," the receptionist replied, trying to be helpful.

"Thank you. Can I also get your mobile number?"

"I'm sorry. I can't give that to you. We're not allowed to be contacted outside of office hours."

"Okay, I understand." I was not familiar with work-related laws, although I was aware that they were very strict. "Let me know what you find out about the ground transportation company. I just don't understand why they didn't show up today."

"I'm on it," she said. "Lunch will arrive around 11:30 AM. If you have a minute, I'll show you where we will serve the food."

I followed her to the room. It had tables and benches as well as an area for the food to be served.

"This will do just fine," I said. "I'll meet you back here around 11:30 AM."

I headed back to my work area to check email and reconfirm the dinner details for the evening. I didn't need anything else to go wrong. A few minutes later the receptionist came by to let me know that she had finally reached the ground transportation company.

"Why didn't they show?" I asked.

"They decided that they didn't want to pick up the group that early in the morning."

"*What?*" I screamed in my mind. "What kind of *vendor* is this?"

She spoke again and brought me out of my angry thoughts. "I told them that we won't need their services anymore."

49

"That's for sure," I said before she could continue. "Please tell me they won't be charging us."

She confirmed there wouldn't be a charge and continued: "I called the other transportation company, and they have a shuttle available. It will arrive this afternoon promptly at 5:30 PM."

"Thanks for getting the shuttle set up. Fingers crossed that all will go well."

I went back to work and, before I knew it, it was lunch time. I headed up to the room where the food was to be served. The receptionist was setting up.

I looked around and asked, "Where is the rest of the food?"

"I decided that we wouldn't need all the food you had suggested. There is plenty for them to eat. If they want to have a sandwich, they can make one in the kitchen area. We have a refrigerator stocked with food." She said all of this as if it wasn't of any concern.

"But they won't have time to make a sandwich. They only have a short break to grab lunch. Is there any way we can bring the sandwich fixings in here? We also have vegetarians, and I don't see anything for them. What happened to the menu we discussed?"

By this time, I was ready to lose it! This was like a bad dream that just wouldn't end.

The receptionist insisted that everything would be fine. I wish I had her confidence. To me, it was a train wreck, and it felt as if another train was going to pile on top. There wasn't any time to get sandwich fixings or anything else because, at that moment, the attendees entered the room. They looked around and saw the meager meal. One of the attendees asked where the rest of the food was hiding. A few of the German attendees quickly grabbed food, and the others followed.

To say that it was awkward would be an understatement. There were several derogatory comments made, and a few walked out without eating. I felt completely helpless. Had I been in the United States, I would have had additional food on the way. I was beyond frustrated.

Then my boss entered the room.

"I thought you had ordered sandwiches too?" he said with disappointment.

I told him about the fixings in the kitchen area and asked if he'd like me to make him a sandwich. He shook his head "no" and walked out of the room. That was it. I had to turn this around and fast!

I went to the receptionist and asked if she could call a catering company (or give me the number to one) so we could order some protein bars, cookies, and pastries for the afternoon break.

"Let's also have coffee, tea, and sodas available. We'll bring them in the room since some of the attendees didn't eat. Could we also review the menus for the rest of the week? We just can't have this happen again tomorrow."

Once the snacks were ordered and the menus reviewed, I went back to my desk. While I waited for the goodies to be delivered, I checked email. I noticed one from my boss. As I read it, my heart sank. He had clearly pointed out *everything* that had gone wrong that day. He especially stressed his disappointment with the lunch menu and added that many attendees complained to him. I swallowed hard. I had never experienced so many mishaps with one event.

My reply was brief: "I agree with everything you've stated below. I have a surprise on the way for the afternoon break and a new vendor for the shuttle. I've already reviewed the menus for the rest of the week to ensure that we won't have a repeat of today's lunch. I've also reconfirmed the dinner arrangements. I'm doing everything I can to make this better."

The goodies arrived in time for the afternoon break. Several of the attendees joked that all was forgiven since I surprised them with snacks.

"What should we expect for dinner?" they joked. "Will it be anything like our lunch?"

By this time, my sense of humor had returned. "The way this day has been going, your guess is as good as mine!"

They laughed and seemed much happier with the delicious surprise. *Phew* ... it worked.

The shuttle arrived as scheduled, dinner was energetic, and the food was delicious. The rest of the week was uneventful. Even the film crew arrived and set up for the all-hands company meeting without any major interruptions. I was so glad to be returning home that Friday.

I learned later that several of the attendees had placed bets to see if I would last the week. They were certain I'd be heading home on a plane that first day. They also commented on my composure when everything was going wrong. By the end of the week, they were confident that I was the right person for the job.

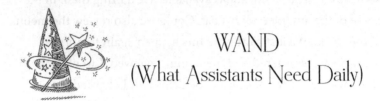

WAND
(What Assistants Need Daily)

✳ Great assistants overcome obstacles by conjuring solutions—just like wizards.

✳ Use composure and diplomacy when situations turn critical. People will watch your behavior to see how you act in stressful situations.

✳ When there is a language barrier, be diligent about the details and overcommunicate to ensure that the information is accurate.

✳ Take ownership for your mistakes, learn from them, don't repeat them, don't blame others, and find alternative solutions.

✳ If you will be traveling to a country unfamiliar to you, take time to learn about their culture and be respectful.

Tough times don't last; tough people do.

—UNKNOWN

Wizards Have Magic beyond the Moon and Stars

HOLD THAT PLANE!

Connections are not always about transportation. The most important connections may be those formed through day-to-day trust and respect. These connections have the biggest payoff.

could feel my heart pounding and hear my heavy breathing.

"I need to get in better shape," I reminded myself as I barreled through the corridors of the airport. I was late for my international flight. Managing my way through security and customs took extra time. The only way I was going to be on my flight was to sprint through the airport at full speed—or at least as fast as I could go with a backpack. It certainly wasn't the same feeling that I had when I ran track in high school. (That was fun; this wasn't.)

I managed to glance at my cell phone to check the time to see if there was any hope of making my flight.

"Faster! I have *got* to go faster if I want to get home tonight!"

Our team had just completed a weeklong strategy meeting at a hotel in the mountains of a beautiful city. We were heading back to the airport for our various flights home. For me, this meant boarding an international flight. It was a two-hour drive from the hotel to the airport. The ground transportation was queued up and ready to go. A last-minute call was added to the CEO's schedule. Since the conversation was sensitive and confidential, the CEO asked that the chief financial officer (CFO) and I ride with him while the other executives traveled in another vehicle.

I checked the time again. We were cutting it close already. Since security lines are unpredictable, I was stressed. Traveling with our CFO meant that the driver had to make a detour through downtown to drop him off at our offices. He was scheduled to work from that location for the day. That added another 15-20 minutes to our trip.

As we dropped off the CFO, I took another peek at the time. I was feeling anxious as it was now 90 minutes before our departure on an international flight. I was trying to remain positive; however, my optimistic attitude was starting to decline.

I wasn't worried about our CEO missing his flight because he had a global entry pass that could get him quickly through airport security and customs. I, however, had to deal with long lines and all the restrictions that come with making your way through airport security.

We arrived with little time to spare. My CEO was on the same flight, and it was becoming clear that he would make it; however, it was highly unlikely that I'd arrive at the gate in time to board. Plus, I had to check my bag, which required more time.

One hour before the flight was scheduled to depart, I recalled air travel options and felt extremely discouraged at the idea of taking a later flight (even if there was one). I cut ahead of the line and asked the ticket agent if I could drop off my luggage as my flight was departing in one hour. Lucky for me, she was kind and attentive and so were the travelers behind me. She quickly printed my info to tag my bag and directed me to the luggage drop area. She added a big "RUSH" sticker so the baggage staff would know to process it quickly.

As soon as I could see that my bag was safely on its way, I darted to the security line. If I had to drag my luggage with me, it would have slowed me down. Checking my luggage would prove to be for my benefit, at least for this flight.

As I approached the security line, panic shot through my veins and down to my toes. The line was long and slow. It didn't help that I'd have to remove my shoes, belt, laptop, cell phone, liquids, and any other items that required special screening. The other executives were at least 15-20 minutes ahead of me.

"Oh! If only I had a global entry pass!" I thought.

I slowly made my way through the screening area.

"Oh, boy! How am I going to get through this mess in time to board my flight?"

I stayed positive, believing that somehow luck and opportunity would come my way as I slowly maneuvered through the long line.

Apparently, as you make your way through security at this airport, there is a designated security officer who makes random checks. It must have been my lucky day because I was the random pick.

The officer looked up at me, and I smiled.

"Is it your lucky day?" he asked.

"Every day is my lucky day, but I suppose that today it is up to you," I said with the utmost confidence.

He grinned even more. "I like your answer. Today *is* your lucky day. You may proceed to security."

I looked at him in total disbelief.

"Hurry! Go and catch your flight," he said with a little chuckle.

I hurried to the line and removed my shoes, belt, and some other items. Then I felt my phone vibrate. It was a text message from my boss:

"We're all at the gate. They've already started boarding. Where are you?"

"I just made it through security and am heading to the customs line," I texted back.

"OK. Let me see if I can stall to give you a little time."

I was curious about the stall tactics and thought, "Would he really do something like that?"

Soon it was my turn in the customs line. I showed the attendant my documentation, including my driver's license and passport. My passport was about nine years old. Back then, my hair was short, and I was a brunette; now, the attendant was staring at a blonde with long hair. Unfortunately, the picture on my license looked the same as my passport picture. He asked questions about what I was doing in their country.

"I'm here on business. Our team just finished a strategy offsite meeting, and I'm the last one to get to the airport. I will most likely miss my flight as I've just learned that the rest of our team has already boarded the plane."

He looked at my passport photo again, commented that he liked my new hairdo better, and said, "Everything looks in order. Run so you don't miss your flight!"

"THANK YOU," I shouted as I looked over my shoulder and sprinted along the corridor.

Another text from my CEO said, "How far away are you? I can't stall much longer. Everyone has boarded the plane, except for me."

"Wow," I thought as I continued my sprint to the gate. "I can't believe he intentionally stalled the plane to allow me time to make the flight!"

I picked up my pace as the gate was at the end of the airport terminal.

I kept thinking, "Boy, am I glad I'm not dragging my suitcase."

I also wondered if my luggage would make it to the plane as I had checked it in right at the cutoff time. That was the least of my worries right now.

I rounded the corner and saw another text: "They've told me that I have to board the plane now. Are you almost here? They are closing the door!"

My heart dropped a little, but I kept going. I was almost there.

Then I saw the attendant pushing the door closed.

I almost shouted, "WAIT FOR ME!"

Was I too late?

As I approached the attendant, I could hear him exchanging conversation on his radio. "We will need to remove the passenger's luggage as she hasn't arrived."

As he finished the sentence, he looked up and saw me.

"Am I too late?"

"Did you check your luggage?"

"Yes, I did!"

He clicked on his radio and gave instructions *not* to remove the luggage as the passenger had just arrived.

"May I have your boarding pass please?"

I handed him the somewhat wrinkled pass.

"Okay. We'll let you through as the door of the plane hasn't been closed yet."

I rushed down the entrance and made a long lunge onto the plane.

As I caught my balance, I gratefully exclaimed, "Thank you so much for keeping that door open!"

It surprised my boss as he was just getting settled on the plane and wasn't expecting me. He gave me a smile and offered a look of relief. *I'd made it!*

I found my way to an aisle seat and glanced around the cabin. I realized that I was the last person to board the plane and had the only open seat left!

I heard a passenger from the back shout, "You must be someone really important for them to hold the plane for you!"

I gave a cursory smile and sighed with relief. I nestled in my seat and quietly grinned with the satisfaction that I had made it.

My boss was my hero that day. I never would have made that flight had he not used his stalling tactics.

WAND
(What Assistants Need Daily)

* If you continuously provide excellent work, when you are in a difficult situation, your boss or coworker will return the favor when you most need it. Wizards will do the same, although you must perform something amazing first.

* Try to build rapport with your executive. It can have surprising results when you least expect it.

* When handling group events, be sure to allow extra time for ground transportation or unexpected delays.

* Although I don't recommend stalling tactics to delay flights, show appreciation and gratitude to your boss or coworker when they do something unexpected.

* Remember to thank your executive or coworker for remembering (and noticing) that you were missing from the group.

* Apply for global entry clearance to spare you having to wait in long lines at the airport.

> Most good relationships are built
> on mutual trust and respect.
>
> —MONA SUTPHEN

Gifted Wizards Have Mind-Reading Abilities

MIND-READER EXPECTATIONS

When an assistant starts a new job, it can be exhausting and stressful while learning new processes and procedures, especially when there are no files or information available to review. Having mind-reading skills would have been a great attribute to get things moving in the right direction!

The first day of my new job as assistant to the CEO had arrived. To get a running start on this new environment, I began looking for old files at my new desk. Since there was no one to train me, I secretly hoped for a book of instructions. Sadly, there was nothing to be found. *Absolutely nothing!* Every file drawer was empty, and the only thing I could find was an outdated binder on my desk, which contained old purchase orders.

"How frustrating!" I said out loud. "I've heard of a paperless environment, but this is ridiculous!"

Not only was the desk empty, the computer didn't have any files on it either. Talk about a challenge!

I thought, "Well, I'd better get busy figuring out processes since we have an upcoming board meeting, and I'm not sure where to start."

I'd handled lots of board material and meetings at previous companies, so I wondered how difficult it could be.

As I visited with staff members, I heard stories about the CEO's previous assistants. Apparently, he had gone through a few assistants over the past several months. What was I getting myself into? From the stories shared, it became clear that the previous assistants were less experienced and were more interested in their social life around the office than they were with the business.

It was important to show the executive team the value of an experienced assistant with a focus around productive meetings. Hopefully my approach would be accepted.

While I was learning about the company culture, its processes, and my role, I started to implement some subtle methods of my own to help make the CEO's office run smoother. My workload was crazy busy, and the board meeting was fast approaching. I had little time to meet with the CEO as he had a busy travel schedule as well as tons of back-to-back meetings.

We finally had a few minutes to discuss the board agenda and material. I felt a little lost for such an incredibly important meeting.

I thought, "You're a high-level assistant with experience and skills. You've done meetings like this hundreds of times, so organizing this one will be a piece of cake!"

At previous companies, I had developed checklists and spreadsheets to track all the details of large meetings. Since I was at a new job, I didn't have this information at my fingertips—at least not yet. With all there was to learn, I was feeling disorganized and somewhat unprepared.

My goal was to have a flawless meeting to show my new CEO that he made the right decision in hiring me. So many questions flooded my mind. I was still unsure about how everything would come together.

"If only I had asked the CEO more questions," I told myself. "Did he think that I had some magic book of instructions?"

I finally pulled myself together and went into laser-focus mode. With a lot of effort, the board package was complete and ready to be shipped. *Success!* I had met the FedEx shipping deadline. The board materials were distributed to the CFO, the general counsel, and most importantly the CEO.

The CEO took a quick look at the material and commented that it was one of the best-organized board books he'd ever seen! I left for the evening and was relieved that everything had finally come together.

I arrived early the next morning to finish a few details before departing for our offsite board committee meetings, which took place the day prior to the board meeting. Our executive team was in their regular weekly staff meeting. Imagine my surprise when the CEO and a few members of his executive team showed up at my desk following the meeting.

The CEO looked very serious. Had I done something wrong? He had my full attention.

With a patronizing voice, he said, "How come all the members of my executive team did not receive a copy of the board material?"

Talk about an awkward and intimidating situation! Three weeks on the job, and the CEO was scolding me in front of the team.

I held my composure and, with extreme confidence, said, "At previous companies, the protocol has been to provide board material to the CFO, the general counsel, and the CEO. Since some of the information is highly confidential, I didn't realize all your staff members needed to receive a copy."

His next comment shocked me when he said, "We have no secrets here. Of course, my staff members receive a copy of the board material. Why wouldn't they? Don't you have some type of instruction book at your desk that details the board meeting process?"

Yikes! He hit my hot button with that comment.

I jumped in with a lofty voice and responded, "Do you think I'm a mind reader?"

With that comment, one of his staff members elbowed the CEO and jokingly said, "Yeah, maybe you should have hired a mind reader."

I must have given him the death stare because he stopped the gesture almost instantly.

I continued speaking to the CEO with a demanding voice. "You never mentioned that all of your staff members should receive copies of the material."

In an instant, I pulled out a piece of blank white paper and opened the empty file drawer. "As you can see, these file drawers are empty. They don't contain any history of what's previously been done in this office. There is no book of instructions, no board-related files … *nothing*! I'm making this up as I go along. I'll be sure to add a note to make copies for all your staff members."

I then directed my focus to the executive staff members who were standing at my desk. "Since the committee meetings begin in a few hours, you obviously won't have material to review this afternoon; however, I'll return this evening to compile the documents. Tomorrow morning, you can pick up your books just before the meeting begins. I apologize for the inconvenience, but, as you can see, we had a little snag in communication."

The CEO gave me a look of aversion, turned on his heels, and walked into his office, shutting the door behind him. The staff members seemed to smile in unison as they walked away.

I couldn't believe that those words came out of my mouth. How could I let my behavior get so out of control—especially in front of the executive team! My credibility and professionalism were at stake. I was terrified that today was going to be my last day. I looked around for an empty box, just in case I needed something in which to put my personal items on my way out the door.

"What do the smiles on the executives' faces really represent?" I thought. "How am I going to recover from this fiasco?"

I made it through the committee meetings with a big knot in my stomach. The board dinner was scheduled shortly after the committee meetings. It was time to approach the CEO to review the wine list for the dinner. I decided that it was also my opportunity to apologize for my outburst earlier that day.

As the CEO reviewed the wine list, I spoke up. "I feel that I owe you an apology for my behavior earlier today. I should have checked with you about who on your staff should have received the material."

The CEO was quiet. I was certain this would be the first and last board meeting I ever organized for him.

As he handed me the wine list, he grinned. "You had every reason to be upset, and you were right to hold me accountable. I can tell the two of us are going to get along just fine. You already know how to manage me. And, by the way, I'm new at this too, but I can be trained. No need to apologize. Everything is fine."

What a relief! I realized that the smiles on the faces of the executive team earlier that day represented their relief in knowing that the new assistant could manage the CEO's boisterous behavior and somewhat unpredictable personality.

WAND
(What Assistants Need Daily)

* Wizards have the confidence to speak up. Follow their lead.

* Develop master checklists and spreadsheet templates and always keep samples available. As needed, edit the checklist to fit the style and culture of each new company assignment.

* Reach out to your network when you are feeling overwhelmed or discouraged. There are so many amazing assistants who have had similar experiences and are anxious to share their ideas.

* Don't be afraid to speak up and share your ideas, especially in a new environment.

* Ask questions. Just because one technique works for someone you've supported in the past, it doesn't mean that it works well for your new or future executive.

✱ If you ever find yourself in a position of conflict in a public area, and you feel uncomfortable or awkward, suggest having the conversation in a more private setting. Who needs the entire office to overhear an awkward conversation?

✱ If you have a conversation that goes badly, be humble and have the courage to apologize.

✱ Seek out people who can help you learn company culture.

✱ Find resources and share ideas to successfully work with your executive.

It is not enough to have a good mind;
the main thing is to use it well.

—RENÉ DESCARTES

Wizards Foretell without Apparatus

INTUITION, INTERVIEWS, AND GUMPTION

Exhibiting gumption and intuition convince a CEO that the assistant's input can provide additional insight when hiring high-level candidates.

Our company was searching for a C-level executive for a newly formed confidential position. Although I wasn't new to the assistant profession, I was new to the company with only about three months of exposure and experience. During those first three to six months, I worked long hours to ramp up and quickly learn my CEO's work style, priorities, goals, initiatives, and processes as well as the company culture. Those first months can be challenging as you attempt to build relationships, learn all the processes and procedures, and understand your executive's expectations.

To help paint the picture, let me describe my CEO. He could be highly productive, meticulous about details, very organized, super smart, and pleasant and engaging with others. He expected perfection (right down to the appearance and tidiness of the office) and exuded tons of confidence and positivity. He was direct in his communication, always diplomatic, quick to analyze situations, and deadline driven. He expected perfection from his senior management team, which included me, and there was extreme pressure to get the details right. It was a fast-paced environment full of challenges and interruptions.

This was a global company with an executive team dispersed in multiple locations. Trying to align schedules for meetings meant that someone always had to be flexible.

During the first week on the job, we had a face-to-face board meeting. During this meeting, introductions among our board members and senior executives were made. I made an extra effort to build rapport with everyone over the next three months. I knew that I would need their help and support to keep our CEO and the company moving in the right direction. My job depended on it! Taking the time to do this paid back tenfold.

Now for the rest of the story:

Our CEO had been searching for a specific candidate for a newly created senior-level position. He thought he had found *the one,* but—after a long, drawn-out offer process—the candidate declined. It was obvious to me that he was extremely let down. He had spent a lot of effort and time with the candidate.

"I know you're disappointed about the candidate deciding not to join us," I said with tons of empathy. "Perhaps you could look at it this way: That candidate wasn't *the one.* We just need to wait for someone better."

Although I really did believe this, I was also doing my best to cheer him up.

Soon we were back on track with a new round of candidates to interview. As I have done in the past, I greeted the candidates in the lobby and engaged them in conversation. As research shows, you can learn a lot about a person in the first five to 10 minutes, and I did not lose a minute of that precious time. My experience and performance reviews mention that, when it comes to people, I have excellent intuitive skills.

We had a few candidates meet with my boss, but we still hadn't found the ideal one. I greeted the next candidate of the day. As we exchanged pleasantries, I took her to the break room for coffee. It wasn't so much about our conversation as it was about how we interacted. She was engaged, positive, and interested in me and my role, the company, our CEO, and his team. She asked great questions in those few short minutes. Best of all, she was interesting with a fun sense of humor. During our short exchange, I had no gauge on her skills or abilities, although I guessed that it had already been established. Nevertheless, I knew that she would blend well with our team. We couldn't let this one get away!

I excused myself, leaving her in the conference room with a fabulous view of Silicon Valley, and headed back to my desk. That day, I had what some people call "gumption." I stopped by our CEO's desk to let him know that the candidate was ready.

With a big smile on my face, I quickly added, "She's the *one*." Believe it or not, those words came out of my mouth—just like that!

Since my relationship with the CEO was still new, and our CEO hadn't had much experience with my so-called intuition, the look on his face said volumes. It was full of surprise.

If I had to describe it in words, it would be, "*What?* Where did you come up with *that*? How do *you* know what type of executive I need?"

He was speechless.

After a few seconds, he finally said, "What makes you think she's the one?"

I'd already said too much and didn't want to give him any more preconceived impressions, so I simply responded, "Go find out for yourself. We can compare notes later."

With that, he went off to the conference room with a bewildered look on his face. About an hour or so passed before he emerged from the interview. The CEO had a bounce in his step and a *big* smile.

As he approached my desk, he said, "You're right! I think she's the one too!"

We chatted briefly about how we came to that conclusion. Although he had examined her skills and experience at a deeper level, we agreed that her interpersonal skills and good nature would be a great fit for our team. The company culture needed someone like this.

We discussed the next steps to get her in front of our senior team. Within a week, the interviews had been completed, and all the feedback was in. *She was the one for us!* An offer was extended, she accepted, and she had a great impact in driving several initiatives to help the company scale to the next level.

This scenario gained my CEO's trust. As a result, we implemented a new practice: I would now greet candidates, get them settled into the conference room, and spend a few minutes talking with them. Following the interview, the CEO and I would compare notes and first impressions to determine the next steps for visiting candidates. This process made me feel more like a business partner than a guest greeter as the CEO truly valued my input.

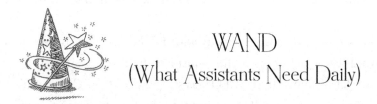

WAND
(What Assistants Need Daily)

✳ Wizards use intuition. Try to fine-tune your intuition to help you make decisions.

✳ First impressions are critical. Although it's possible to make a good impression down the road, don't lose the chance to make a lasting impression.

✳ Rely on your intuition to help you make decisions. When using your intuition, be sure to draw upon your experience to weigh all the facts.

✳ Learn your executive's style along with the company culture so you can provide valued feedback and input.

✳ Always treat those around you with kindness no matter what title they hold. Practicing this attribute will provide you with influencing opportunities in your career.

There are only three things that can make your dreams come true: your thoughts, your words, and your actions.

—MIKE DOOLEY

Wizards Fear Few Things

MAY I INTERRUPT?

There is a fine line between being respectful and gaining respect by duress. By being aware of those in the room, assistants can diffuse a situation that saves a reputation and shows courage and mutual respect.

Our product managers had scheduled a review meeting with our CEO, which was done monthly to keep the team and the CEO up to date on new product developments, timelines, deadlines, announcements, new product designs, fixes, and anything else related to our products.

This meeting agenda included several items, so the CEO requested that I step into the room and scribe key takeaways. I quickly grabbed my pen, notebook, and laptop, and surveyed the room for the best place to sit. By this time, the team had already gathered in his office. I thought it best to sit at his desk and take notes to avoid creating any distractions.

The meeting progressed through the agenda. Finally, it was time to discuss the last item. The team was having product development issues, which would cause a significant delay in the product delivery timeline, and additional urgent issues needed to be discussed.

The product manager who gave the update was direct and to the point. Although that was the right approach and preferred style of our CEO, the news delivered was far more crucial than he had anticipated. The CEO felt that several items should have been escalated to his attention weeks earlier. It got to a point that the CEO had heard enough. It was as though someone had waved a red flag at a raging bull.

As I was finalizing the last action item, I heard the CEO yelling at someone. I stopped taking notes and looked up to see my boss inches away from the product manager's face. To put it mildly, he was intense, shouting, and agitated. I don't think I've ever heard as many swear words as I heard that day.

Glancing around the room, I sensed the body language of each attendee. There was no eye contact with anyone; everyone's head was down, and bodies seemed to shrink as the yelling escalated. No one was going to interrupt this tirade for fear of being the next one under attack.

I sensed that safety had vanished from the room and knew that they wouldn't get anything accomplished until the CEO's rant was done, but when would that be? He was on a roll, and it would be career limiting to interrupt.

Even so, that little voice in my head nudged me. "Speak up! You have to say something!" If I interrupted, the risk was *huge*. "Choose your words carefully, Linda."

The CEO took a breath.

Like rushing waters from a waterfall, words began to come out of my mouth. "May I interrupt?"

Instantly, all heads were turned, and everyone was looking at me with shock and dismay—or perhaps it was relief that someone had stopped the rant. Before anyone could say a word, I proceeded.

"I believe we all understand that this information is disturbing. I mean no disrespect to you or the team, but I am wondering if you could cease with the swearing and focus on the next steps and action items."

I held my breath for what seemed like hours. I had interrupted the CEO during an intense conversation. I was sure this wasn't going to end well for me. The attention in the room had gone from no eye contact to all eyes on me.

The team's body language was saying, "Are you *crazy*? Now he'll be yelling at you! Why are you *doing* this?"

I kept my composure. After a few moments of silence, the CEO took a deep breath and relaxed. It was completely unexpected. I was ready for a verbal beating. Instead, the CEO did something very noble.

He turned, looked at me, and said, "Linda's right. I'm beyond upset. I'm furious, disappointed, and more. I'll stop swearing, but I need you all to understand that this situation is critical to our business. It's not good. You've failed to meet our critical deadline, and we need to figure out as a team how we will proceed to get back on track."

The environment in the room completely changed. It seemed as if everyone could breathe again. Making that comment helped the attendees feel safe. They went back to dialog and discussed the next steps to get things moving forward.

I finished the notes as the meeting wrapped up and headed back to my desk. The CEO passed me, caught my eye, and nodded. He never said a word nor did we discuss what happened.

I believe the nod was his way of saying, "Thank you for having my back." Maybe he was thanking me for having the courage to speak up in such an awkward situation.

Later in the day, a few of the attendees separately stopped by my desk. The general messages were, "That was a brave thing you did in that meeting." They further commented that they were sure the CEO was going to kick me out of the room, but he didn't.

I gained a lot of respect from the CEO and his team. I too gained a new level of respect for the CEO as a leader. Instead of attacking me when I interrupted him, he realized the severity of the situation. With that short pause, his reaction brought safety and respect back to the room. Somehow, he realized that his behavior was heading in the wrong direction. Instantly, he understood that the relationships of those in the room were more important than the embarrassment I may have caused him. His reaction and respect helped me gain credibility with him and the team and showed the true leader that he had become.

WAND
(What Assistants Need Daily)

* Assistants and wizards are gifted with courage and clever magic. Don't miss an opportunity to shine.

* Fear is an illusion. Speak up when conversations become awkward.

* If someone's body language tells you that they are no longer engaged in the conversation, respectfully share your thoughts.

* Relationships matter. Remember to behave in a way that you want to be treated.

* Prepare a few phrases to use when conversations turn awkward. Acknowledge the situation.

* Showing respect will give you credibility and the trust of your coworkers.

* If you catch yourself yelling during a conversation, show your leadership skills by examining your true motives. You will gain more respect if you admit your bad behavior.

> True self-respect, being very
> different from false pride, leads
> inevitably to respecting others.
>
> —VIRGINIA MOORE

Wizards Keep Secrets

THE HAIRCUT

Having courage and taking a risk to do a little image building for the CEO can be scary. Would this risk be a career-limiting move?

It was a day of back-to-back meetings. The CEO was tucked away for a few hours. I was reading through email when, out of the corner of my eye, I saw the corporate communications director approaching my cube. He peeked in my executive's office to see if he was there, and then he turned to me.

"I need your help," he said in a secretive voice.

"Of course."

"It's kind of a strange request."

"Okay. You have my attention," I answered, intrigued.

My boss was someone who didn't spend a lot of time grooming his hair. In fact, it had grown quite long and often looked disheveled. He was one of those lucky men with lots of thick hair. He was often teased by staff members about the length of it. In fact, I vividly remember when he received quite a bit of taunting from several departments as he was scheduled to be on television in a few weeks.

People would stop at my desk and ask if there was anything that I could do about his hair. I had offered to set up appointments and even scheduled a few; however, from time to time, he would get tied up in some meeting and those appointments were rescheduled or cancelled.

During this time of consistent nagging about his hair, he stopped by my desk and asked, "Linda, what do you think about my hair? Do you think it's too messy and too long?"

I didn't hesitate. "It looks great. You're lucky to have such beautiful, thick hair. Plus, it really doesn't matter what I think. It's your hair."

"I knew I liked you," he smiled, feeling smug.

Then I added, "I guess it depends on whether you'd like the investors to take you seriously and possibly see an increase in the stock price."

That comment caught his attention. "What do you mean?"

"Well, from my experience, it seems that executives who are well groomed, especially their hair, tend to be taken more seriously. Research proves this. It isn't fair, but if you plan to appear on television, it's best if you are well groomed. That message is important. Whether you like it or not, you represent the company."

By the look on his face, I'm sure he wanted to take back his previous comment about liking me. He turned and walked to his office.

So how should I help our director without causing an awkward incident with our CEO? After brainstorming, the director suggested that we bring a hair stylist to the office. He knew someone who he thought would be willing to help us with this plan.

"I like that idea," I offered. "It sounds risky and could be career-limiting for me, but we have to do something to get his hair under control. A trim could make all the difference."

He was shocked and amazed at my response. His impression of me was a person with a conservative approach. He couldn't believe that I'd be willing to take the risk. We checked the calendar for times to schedule the haircut and added what my boss thought would be a catch-up meeting with the communications director.

"Thank you," he said with a sigh of relief. "I really think this is the best way to handle it."

I crossed my fingers and hoped this minor deception we were playing on the CEO would not lead to a dismissal or a loud, stern lecture about abusing my power and his trust.

The day arrived for the secret meeting. I walked with my boss to his office. I had already set up an area with all the tools needed for a haircut, including the hair stylist. As I opened the door, he had a stunned look on his face.

"What's going on?"

With a sweep of my arm and all the confidence I could muster, I told him, "Go ahead. Have a seat. It's time for a trim and an updated look. I know you've been busy, so I took the liberty of setting up an onsite stylist. It's up to you how much she cuts."

He turned and gave me the death stare; however, as he did that, he let out a little chuckle. I was hoping that laugh was going to provide some mercy later.

As I closed the door, I caught a glimpse of him sitting down. The hair stylist put a wrap around him, and he was still quietly chuckling. At least he didn't immediately dismiss me and her. There was still hope that I'd have a job tomorrow!

About 20 minutes later, he emerged from his office. Although he didn't have much of a haircut, the stylist had given him a smoother look—more professionally groomed.

"What do you think?" he said as he stepped up to my cube. (At least he was still talking to me.)

"*Much* better."

"Who else was in on these shenanigans? Did the communications department put you up to this?"

Busted! I explained our good intentions without throwing anyone under the bus. We all thought it would be worth a try to see if updating our CEO's image would make a difference in people's perception about the company and our CEO. It's always good to have a nudge in the right direction.

Of course, he couldn't help himself. He had to make his way over to the communications department to hassle them a bit and, more than likely, show off his new hairstyle. A week or so later, he made his appearance on television. He seemed more confident, or maybe I just wanted to believe that a little trim and style could have a significant impact.

Our stock increased. I'm sure it had something to do with the company's performance, although I'd like to think a little CEO branding and styling from our team also made a difference.

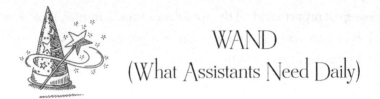

WAND
(What Assistants Need Daily)

✳ Use your humor and charm, like wizards, and don't share secrets.

✳ First impressions are critical when communicating company information. Find ways to help build your company brand. Sometimes it includes carefully providing advice to your manager about his/her appearance.

✳ Empower yourself to make decisions in situations that require you to take some risks.

✳ Learn your executive's style along with the company culture to provide valued feedback and input.

✳ To learn and grow, take risks. More opportunities will be presented.

If you are not willing to risk the unusual,
you will have to settle for the ordinary.

—JIM ROHN

Wizards Know How and Whom to Trust

ELEGANT DINING

Attending an offsite meeting and an extravagant kick-off dinner feels good. Well, that was the plan until reality reared its ugly head.

interviewed for a position with the CEO of a large software company. During our meeting, the CEO explained that the board tasked him with turning the company around from a downward spiral to a position of growth. To accomplish this goal, he needed an assistant as passionate and dedicated as he was. This assistant would need to put in hard work to get the job done.

From my experience working with turnaround CEOs, I knew there was nothing more satisfying than seeing a company rise from the brink of failure to the height of success. There would be some unpopular decisions ahead for him as organizational changes are difficult to maneuver. I was the person who could help him achieve this tremendous undertaking. He agreed, and I became his assistant.

The company was losing sales and profitability at an alarming rate and, understandably, the CEO was under a great deal of pressure. To bring management to terms with the company's failing position, he determined that it was time to get their attention and unite on a strategy. Knowing that he could not do it alone, he hired a consultant to help him arrange an offsite meeting with his executive team and about a dozen other key individuals. With the consultant's input, the CEO took the lead and developed the agenda. I was in charge of putting together the logistics and portions of the communication details. Since the CEO was trying to make an impact during this meeting, he advised me to keep all the details confidential. Although I saw several versions of the proposed plan, they were intentionally left obscure.

The consultant and I identified a location and ordered the catering for the all-day meeting. In addition, I helped the attendees with room reservations, travel plans, and any last-minute logistics. During the all-day meeting, I would be onsite, handling administrative needs, scribing key notes, and monitoring breakout activities.

We identified a meeting place that met the CEO's specifications in downtown San Francisco: the majestic Fairmont Hotel. Due to the economic downturn for technology companies, the rates were unbelievably cost effective. Their Fountain Room, known for its breathtaking scenic view and gourmet dining, would be the backdrop for the kick-off dinner.

The CEO told me to ensure that the dinner would be exceptional. "Spare no expense. Order china, beautiful table decorations, wine glasses, and silverware. I'll personally take care of the dinner menu for that night."

I was somewhat surprised to hear him say, "Spare no expense." He was decidedly conservative when it came to business expenditures, and I knew the company's negative financial condition. For the CEO to make such a fuss over this dinner, I assumed that he would be delivering an extremely powerful message to the team.

The day of the event arrived. About an hour before I was scheduled to depart for San Francisco to make sure that everything was in order, the CEO gave me an urgent project that would take several hours to complete. He needed it for the meeting the next day. This additional assignment meant that I wouldn't get to San Francisco in time to attend the dinner. I really wanted to be in attendance and hear the powerful messages being delivered during the kick-off event.

I couldn't hide my disappointment. "You mean I'll miss dinner at the Fountain Room in San Francisco?"

He smiled half-heartedly in my direction as he hurried out the door. "Don't come to San Francisco tonight, Linda. Just drive up in the morning. I'll call you from the car and give you more details."

I was feeling totally deflated at being excluded. I was going to miss the kick-off dinner with the team, the spectacular view from the Fountain Room, *and* a delectable dinner! At least that's what I anticipated. Maybe I could finish the project and make it to San Francisco in time for dessert!

As my mind wandered in that direction, the phone rang. As promised, it was the CEO calling from the car.

I picked up immediately and tried not to whine. "Are you *sure* you want me to stay behind?"

Apparently, he thought he owed me an explanation for his abrupt departure and last-minute project.

"Linda," he said, "I am going to share the purpose of this offsite meeting. It is highly confidential, so you need to keep these details to yourself."

He told me that the elegant dinner that evening would not be what it seemed. Although the management team would have a beautiful venue and the appearance of an elegant dinner, the only food being served that night would be bread and water.

"We don't deserve any meal better than that," he continued. "We need to focus, and we'll start by giving them a meal that matches our current performance. Our situation is serious, and we need to agree on our new strategy. This wake-up call will help identify the team players for the new organization. Linda, you deserve an elegant dinner, not bread and water. Come join us in the morning for the all-day session."

Although it made me feel much better, I felt bad for him. It was going to be a brutal evening. I felt a sense of relief, knowing that he trusted me with the big picture and respected me enough to shield me from his harsh showdown.

I learned the next morning that the CEO was true to his word: It was a wake-up call for the team. He had Elton John's song, "Funeral for a Friend," played just before he announced the menu of bread and water. Then he told the attendees that, if they were still hungry after dinner, they could order room service or go out to eat; however, he'd better not see any of it on an expense report.

They heard him loud and clear. Would they commit to the new organization plan and strategy by the end of the offsite meeting, or would they choose to depart and make room for an unidentified replacement, so the company could execute the new plan?

There were several grim faces among the management group the next morning, and the team understood the serious nature and importance of the next steps for the company. At the end of the offsite meeting, it was clear that a few executives would not be staying. Their departure was amicable, and the search began to find executives to take on the newly assigned responsibilities. The new team collaborated and executed with a successful outcome.

As the CEO's business partner and trusted assistant, I had the good fortune to experience the transformation of a struggling company into a profitable one. I found it truly impressive that the CEO managed this feat during one of the most turbulent and difficult times in the tech industry. He developed a culture of trust, integrity, mutual respect, and collaboration due to his high work ethic, integrity, and commitment. These are important ingredients for a successful company and leader. *Lucky me!*

WAND
(What Assistants Need Daily)

❄ Show confidence and trust even when things don't seem transparent.

❄ Don't be too quick to second-guess your executive's decisions. Details of the "big picture" can't always be shared.

❄ Remember that the importance of offsite meetings is to focus on business. It isn't all about an elegant dinner or an inspiring venue (although that certainly makes it feel special).

❄ Understanding the importance of confidentiality is critical to becoming a confidential sounding board.

❄ When you persevere during difficult times, amazing mentorships can be formed.

❄ Identify leaders with integrity who know how to maneuver through times of adversity. They can teach you critical leadership skills.

❄ When you exemplify qualities of trust, these will be the key to building a strong partnership with your executive.

❄ Don't be quick to jump to conclusions without having all the facts.

Man lives more by affirmation than by bread.

—VICTOR HUGO

Wizards Are Natural Philosophers

UNDERSTANDING QUEEN BEE

This story discovers some of the best techniques for maneuvering in a new environment when you are working with challenging people.

Here it was: the end of an intense first week on the job working for the CEO of a Silicon Valley company. My head was swirling with information. Connecting the dots about who handled what was overwhelming. Now, I had to keep it all straight.

One item of importance was a request from the CEO to schedule a critical meeting with several members of the leadership team. Due to strict corporate regulations, I was challenged with getting all required participants to this meeting in person. Conference calls, videos, or substitutes would not be permitted—only the required attendee. This task was made more tedious due to a specific three-week window to schedule it.

After several email exchanges with various assistants, a suitable date and time were identified. Meeting planning is very much like airway traffic control: There are always more planes to land than a landing strip to put them on. Before confirming this meeting, there was one meeting that required a reschedule. Reworking the department meeting with one of our large organizations would be required.

Though this task was an arduous request, I thought, "How hard could it be to move this meeting?"

The assistant (we'll call her Claudia), who originally organized this meeting, was out of the office due to a medical-related illness, so I hadn't met her yet. An alternate assistant was filling in during Claudia's absence. The alternate assistant thought that moving the meeting wouldn't be a problem; however, she would double-check with Claudia once she returned to the office the following Monday. The week's events now ended. It was time to rest my mind and enjoy the weekend, especially now that the meeting details seemed to be settled.

Since I hadn't officially met Claudia, I was eager to connect with her as soon as she returned. On Monday morning, I arrived to see that she was already in the office, busily making calls and talking with people. She sat near me, so I could easily hear most of her interactions. I was busy with the CEO's schedule and figured we would catch up once she finished and my boss was off to his morning meetings.

As I worked, another department assistant passed by my desk.

"I see she's back," she said with a slightly sarcastic tone.

I smiled.

As I interacted with the different assistants and executives during my first week, whenever Claudia's name was mentioned, they would almost *cringe*. Even their body language mimicked that word, and I would see images of Cruella de Vil from *101 Dalmations*.

"She's a real challenge and really intense. Once you meet her, you'll see what I mean," some said.

When Claudia's name was mentioned, conversations would pause, and there would be a sudden hush in the room. They would glance at each other, as if each one wanted to say something. Then, nothing would be said, as if there was an impending curse and they knew that they'd all turn to stone if they did. What was it about this assistant? I was eager and terrified to meet her.

After a few hours, Claudia passed my desk as if I were invisible and planted herself in the CEO's office.

"Your new assistant has scheduled a meeting right on top of one of our critical department meetings!" she shouted.

I suppose he was used to her outbursts. Instead of shooing her out of his office, he turned to her and responded, "Okay, we will move our meeting."

Off she went in a huff.

As she passed my cubicle, she turned to me, leaned into my cube, and said, "How *dare* you try to schedule a meeting during one of my critical meetings. Don't even *think* about it!"

Off she went, back to her cube, with the satisfaction of knowing that she had shown me who was Queen Bee in that department.

I was unable to mutter a response because my mouth was open from the shock that an assistant would behave like that in the workplace. I was still reeling about the situation hours later. How was I going to recover? I still hadn't officially met Claudia and trying to have a conversation now would be awkward. To regain dignity, respect, and credibility as well as develop a productive relationship with Claudia, I would need a strategy.

"What makes her tick?" I wondered.

I was replaying the scene in my head all day long. It was clear that our CEO didn't want to be bothered; he just wanted us to get along and to get things done. I stopped by his office to update him on a few items and give him details about some calls and upcoming meetings.

"I guess things didn't go so well with you and *Claudia* this morning," he said with a giggle.

I was still learning his personality, so I wasn't sure how to take the comment.

"She's a really good assistant, and the two of you will need to work closely together. I hope you're up for the challenge of finding a way to get things done without constant outbursts like that."

Ouch! I was hoping for a little mentoring and support from the CEO. It was clear that he wasn't going to offer any advice. I was on my own with this difficult situation. I was concerned that I hadn't made a great impression with the CEO. I felt like my credibility and likeability traits were being compromised. I was out to prove that I was up for a challenge and determined to make this assistant my new best friend.

I had been reading some books about influence, communication, and leadership as I was preparing and developing a training class for assistants. My next approach became clear.

Tuesday morning arrived, and I was in the office early. So was Claudia. It was quiet, so I approached her desk.

"Good morning, Claudia."

She glanced up. It was perfectly clear that she wasn't impressed to see me.

"I've been thinking about the face-to-face meeting that we need to schedule. I understand the importance of your meeting as well as the timing. I wonder if I could ask for your input on some of the scenarios I think might work for both of us."

She must have been interested because she didn't interrupt.

I explained the various scenarios, asked for her feedback, and ended with this question: "I'd like your input on what you think works best."

It was as if I had used magic words. Her body language changed from unapproachable to engaging. We talked about the scenarios and meeting requirements, the attendees, and our feelings of stress about how nearly impossible it felt to juggle all the meeting criteria.

"I like your ideas, Linda. I appreciate you taking the time to get my point of view and input. You seem to genuinely care about my situation too. I can tell that you and I are going to get along great. I can move my meeting a few hours as we discussed."

I walked back to my cube and was surprised. Could it really be that simple? She wanted to be heard, acknowledged, and valued for the insight she had learned over the years in that role.

She told me later that, after our conversation, she went into her executive's office and said, "Finally! They hired someone who actually values input from others."

I wish I could tell you that there never was another outburst; however, after some time, they did decrease. Our relationship grew into a friendship, and our interactions got easier every day.

About a year after working with Claudia, we reflected on our first encounter. She told me that, before I had arrived, she felt her input had never been acknowledged or considered. She felt that decisions were made without any consideration for how it might impact her, the team, and the meeting schedule. She especially appreciated not hearing the words, "Well, I work for the CEO, and that's what he wants, so you'll just have to make adjustments." She felt disrespected when she heard those types of comments.

Managing such high-level meetings meant that changes were often difficult and rarely practical; however, knowing that I genuinely valued her input helped our productivity and influenced her behavior with the whole department. It was clear that everyone was benefiting from Claudia's much-improved demeanor and team spirit. It caused her to be more considerate and open with information, and this shared knowledge increased all our successes. It also made her think twice when she had to make major changes. This department's assistants took great care when scheduling, and now, with improved team effort, everyone was able to benefit.

Our relationship could have been one of competing and comparing. I'm glad it worked out to be long lasting.

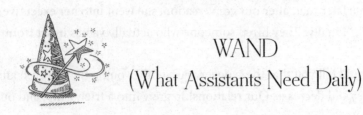

WAND
(What Assistants Need Daily)

* Build exceptional abilities, techniques, and strategies to be a wise and gracious assistant.

* Take time to listen and acknowledge others who have experience and can provide critical information.

* Genuinely interact with people and develop a professional relationship of trust.

* Don't use the inherent power of your title or role to get your way.

* When conversations turn critical, don't make it about you. Find out what makes that person tick.

* Many coworkers will provide you with information about their relationships with other people in the office. Don't jump to conclusions before doing your own due diligence.

* Learn how people think and feel, what inspires them, and how they may act in a situation.

All have their worth and each
contributes to the worth of the others.

—J.R.R. TOLKIEN

Wizards Conjure Up Clever Ideas

PHOTO-SHY CEO

When a company is nominated to receive a prestigious award, the team soon learns that their CEO is photo shy and not interested in participating in a photo shoot.

Our company was nominated for a prestigious award from a prominent magazine, and there was lots of excitement around this news. If we won, it would give our company and the CEO great exposure. Our corporate communications group was abuzz, busily pulling together the details as the deadline was fast approaching to submit the award information.

I was hyperfocused on a project with a deadline and didn't hear our director of communications approach my desk.

Before I could say a word, he blurted out, "I desperately need your help!"

"What's up?" I responded with the same level of excitement.

He had just learned that, as part of the potential magazine award, our CEO would need to do a photo shoot. If our company became the winner (or one of the top five winners), we would need to include photos. Specifically, they required a current photo of our CEO for the magazine cover.

"A *current* photo?"

We both knew that would be a challenge. Our CEO *hated*—and I mean HATED—to have his picture taken. In fact, he was so camera shy that, when I met him at my interview, I didn't recognize him from the website photo. It was truly outdated.

Since I love a challenge, I said in my most confident tone, "I'll talk to the CEO. I'm sure he'll make an exception for this important occasion."

I must have been convincing as the director walked away, looking as if a heavy load had been lifted from him.

I found a few minutes to talk to my boss about our situation and the urgency to put together a photo shoot for him and the magazine.

"Nope," he said as if he had a choice in the matter.

"No photo shoot?" I asked with bewilderment.

"That's right. I'm not doing a photo shoot. I *hate* taking pictures. I'm sure they'll figure something out."

I walked back to my desk in shock. I just couldn't believe that he wouldn't say "yes" to what I felt was a great opportunity to profile the company and him. Perhaps I spoke too soon when I promised the director that I'd handle getting our CEO to buy in to the photo shoot.

Off I went to our communications team to bring them the bad news. We huddled and brainstormed for a new plan and came up with some ideas. We all agreed that, if the photo shoot were to take place in a location of interest to the CEO, we just might have some success.

I headed back to talk to the CEO, determined to influence him about the new ideas. It took some creative conversation—and a little arm twisting—but he finally agreed to one idea. I worked with the team to quickly make the arrangements.

Our CEO loved hockey. We pooled our resources and contacts at the nearby stadium and miraculously pulled together a photo shoot for the next day. Although we were relieved to be able to check that stressful item off our list, we were still on pins and needles until the photos were ready and worthy for the media.

The next day brought its own challenges. As we neared the time for the CEO's departure to the stadium, he had some pressing matters and advised us that he just couldn't get away. The photo shoot would have to wait. Was he kidding? How in the world would we meet the deadline if we couldn't get our CEO to the photo shoot?

I sadly picked up the phone and told the communications team the bad news. Although I sensed the disappointment in the director's voice, we hadn't given up yet. Once again, we were back to brainstorming. Time was running short and so was our patience. If we received the award, how would it look with a blank photo on the front of the magazine? We discussed different strategies and off we went to fine-tune the details.

I was becoming a little anxious about the deadline, and then I had an idea. A few months earlier, the CEO's glasses had broken. He had a few samples that he brought to the office. He wanted to get input before he made his final selection. During the next week, he surveyed almost everyone who came near his office as well as those who met with him throughout the week. Soon it became the joke in the office.

One executive was especially clever. During a meeting to review some important topics, a presentation was shared. Each slide contained a picture of the CEO with all sorts of wild pairs of glasses in different shapes, sizes, and colors. Of course, the executive used the old, outdated picture for the presentation. It was hilarious. I needed to find that presentation—and fast!

After a few calls, I located the slides and quickly went to work printing a few of my favorite ones. Then, I taped one of the pictures to the CEO's office door. When he arrived, I could hear him chuckle.

"Oh, good," I thought. "He thinks it's funny."

As he entered his office, he found a few more pictures. One was posted on his computer, another on his desk, and still another on his phone.

"All right," he said. "What's with all these crazy pictures?"

"Are you in a good mood?" I asked.

"That depends," he said, still grinning.

"I just wanted to make sure you knew that we didn't need to worry about the photo shoot. We can use those pictures for the cover of the magazine."

I breathed a sigh of relief when he chuckled some more.

"Okay, I get it. Set up the photo session. I'll do it."

That's what I was hoping to hear! I gave the communications team the news and, of course, I had to share the story with them.

This time, we kept the photo shoot simple. We had a beautiful campus, and the weather cooperated. All the photos were shot onsite, and everything went as planned. The CEO's picture turned out great. Not only did we have something worthy for the press, we also had an updated photo for our company website.

The day arrived to announce the winner. It was an incredible day of celebration. *We won!* We were happy (and relieved) that we had gone through all that trouble to get photos taken. Not only did it provide some amazing pictures, it saved us from having to use the pictures of the CEO with all those crazy glasses!

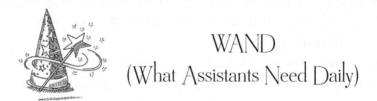

WAND
(What Assistants Need Daily)

✳ When a critical deadline is approaching, use your creativity, resourcefulness, and teamwork to come up with a plan of action.

✳ Take a risk and use humor along with creativity to resolve difficult situations.

✳ Make sure the situation and the timing are appropriate to ensure that your plan doesn't backfire.

✳ Sometimes it's important to act before your executive changes his/her mind.

❋ If you have exhausted all your ideas and resources, brainstorm with coworkers or friends to come up with new ideas and a backup plan.

❋ Don't underestimate your power of positive influence.

❋ Even the best organized plans may fail or must be cancelled, postponed, or changed. Don't give up! Keep brainstorming and using creative ideas to achieve a successful outcome.

Acting on a good idea is better
than just having a good idea.

—ROBERT HALF

Wizards Know People of Influence and High Stature

IT'S ALL ABOUT WHOM YOU KNOW

A simple question opens doors that seemed impossibly locked. The value of a network with finesse and example is the outcome.

I worked in a physically open environment and could usually tune out all the "white noise" around me. The door to my executive's office was typically closed when he was on the phone. For one call, he must not have felt the need for privacy as he left the door open. I sat near his office and could overhear his conversation.

"I need to find a Finland contact who can introduce me to executives and firms in that area to help us expand our market."

I wasn't sure who he was talking to, but I immediately thought, "Contacts in Finland? I can help!"

I was new to the company, and I wasn't yet sure if my executive would value my opinion. What he may not know is that I had been in Silicon Valley for many years and had built a large network of resources.

I took a chance.

After his call was completed, I went to his office before he could make another call or check his email.

"I heard your conversation," I said. "I think I can help you find a Finland contact. Tell me more about what you need."

At first, he gave me a look as if to say, "What can *you* possibly do for *me*?"

I thought, "Boy, do I have a lot to teach him about the power of my network!"

I didn't let that stop me because I knew I could help. I worked at a previous company that did some business in Finland. We quickly discussed more details about his request. I went back to my desk to email my former employer. I was eager to prove that I could help him in other ways besides scheduling meetings and handling travel.

My former executive was happy to help. Within a few days, he put me in touch with some of his contacts. I arranged a call with my executive and, within a week, some face-to-face meetings took place. Within a few months, the Finland contact arranged for other meetings as well as a spot on a panel at a high-profile conference event in the Finland area. That led to scheduling other meetings with significant firms. The conference organizers also assisted in selecting a lineup of meetings.

If I had never asked that simple question, many new opportunities may not have appeared. That introduction increased my credibility and brought potential new business to the company. It helped with business development and had the potential to bring in additional revenue.

Building credibility with my boss pushed our business partnership to the next level.

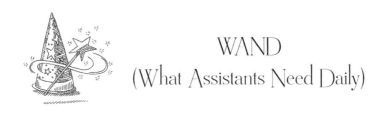

WAND
(What Assistants Need Daily)

✳ Engage your unique magic, and it will be treated with the utmost respect.

✳ Don't underestimate the value of your network and the resources that can help create new opportunities for your executive and company.

✳ Connect your circle of friends. Everyone is connected to someone, so don't be afraid to provide introductions.

✳ You have more influence than you realize. Sometimes it isn't about *what* you know—it's about *whom* you know.

✳ Make simple suggestions or connections to improve your credibility and develop a foundation as a business partner.

✳ Educate others about your value by volunteering for special projects or making suggestions. Your value is comprised of more than your talents and skills.

✳ When you help others connect, you will become the center of influence.

✳ Network all the time—not just when you need a job.

Becoming well known (at least among your prospects and connections) is the most valuable element in the connection process.

—JEFFREY GITOMER

Wizards Handle Situations with the Greatest Care

LISTENING TO INSTRUCTIONS

With a detailed itinerary in hand, the CEO heads out for a long week of travel. In his rush, he neglects to check the correct airport location for his departure. Now what?

was preparing detailed travel information and briefing documents for upcoming customer meetings that our CEO was attending. In reviewing the travel plan with him, I gave specific directions.

"Head to the Reagan National Airport."

I made sure that my instructions were clear as our CEO often departed from Dulles International Airport. His meeting was going to take place a little closer to the Reagan airport, and flight options were better. Before his departure, we reviewed the flight options, and he agreed with the plan. Although our conversation was quick, I was feeling confident about the arrangements. I finalized the tickets, and soon the CEO was on his way.

I was looking forward to a few days to catch my breath as well as handle a few projects that I kept pushing off.

The CEO called to check in before heading to the airport. The meetings had gone well, and he was in a hurry to get home. It had been a busy travel schedule with back-to-back meetings and several different airports.

"I'm with the driver," he explained with a sense of relief.

We reviewed a couple of pending items during his drive to the airport.

The CEO's detailed itinerary ended up with his luggage inside the trunk. Smart phones weren't advanced enough yet, so we were still using the paper system. Once in the car, the CEO told the driver to take him to Dulles airport. I suppose the driver figured that something must have changed. His instructions indicated that he was to take his passenger to the Reagan airport, but he didn't want to argue with the CEO. The driver adjusted his plans without hesitation and delivered the CEO to the new location.

As the CEO stood in the airport searching for the flight that matched his itinerary, he became frustrated because it wasn't listed on the departure board. My phone rang as if it were frustrated too.

He started the conversation with, "I think you must have made a typo on my itinerary. I don't see my flight listed. Can you check it out?"

As I grabbed the folder with the travel details, the thought came to me that he might be at the wrong airport.

Within seconds, I asked, "Are you at the right airport?"

"I'm at Dulles," he said with some disdain.

I replied in a calm voice, "Well, the good news is that the flight information was accurate. The bad news is that you're at the wrong airport."

Before he could say another word, I interjected, "But we can fix this in minutes. Let me get our travel agent on the line."

With that, we found a flight that was leaving within the hour and quickly made the change. He was soon on his way home, and we all had a good laugh about the incident.

WAND
(What Assistants Need Daily)

✳ If you're going to brew like wizards, make sure you have the right ingredients.

✳ When you listen carefully, the details will unfold.

✳ Always be prepared for the unexpected—especially when your executive is traveling.

✳ Maintaining a sense of humor and a calm attitude go a long way towards keeping balance in relationships and sticky situations.

✳ Even when you aren't at fault, maintain an upbeat "We can fix this!" attitude. Tempers will usually remain at bay.

✳ When your instincts speak to you, pay attention. It may be the fastest way to resolve a situation.

> Most people do not listen with the intent to understand; they listen with the intent to reply.
>
> —STEPHEN R. COVEY

Wizards Mend Things When Magic Goes Wrong

"WHAT NUMBER DID YOU CALL?"

This scenario turned around an awkward situation using quick follow-through and a sense of humor.

It was my second week on the job, and I was excited to be working with this CEO. He was known for his impeccable professionalism and high level of integrity, among many other great attributes. In fact, he was a Boy Scout! The bar for performance was set high, which I realized the first minute we met at the interview. Excellent performance would be required for this new role, and I was eager to take on the challenge.

As I settled in, time seemed to move at the speed of light. One day, while reviewing our calendar, the CEO had a scheduled conference call that was fast approaching. This call would be with executives from another company; there was only 10 minutes to spare. I gathered the needed materials, wrote down the conference bridge number, and headed to his office to set up the call.

Within minutes, the CEO rounded the corner. I quickly reviewed the material with him to ensure that he had everything he needed. While he was busily working at his computer, I dialed the number.

The call connected with no problem. A woman with an incredibly sexy and sultry voice answered.

"Hello! I know how to make you *really* happy."

Oh, no! Instead of hearing the recording with the usual instructions about how to reach the operator, mute the call, etc., I somehow had dialed a phone sex line. I sprung from the table, like a young dear startled by an unfamiliar noise.

Imagine my shock as I thought, "This *can't* be the call described in the material I just reviewed!" My heart fell to my feet, and I felt little beads of perspiration form on my forehead. "What have I done? *Now* what?"

I looked at my boss, and then I looked at the phone. I looked at my boss again.

With his glasses perched on the end of his nose, he raised his eyes and said, "Uh, I don't think that's the right number."

I tapped the disconnect button; however, I must have been thrown off my game because it took a few tries to disconnect the call. Then I tried to add some humor to my voice.

"I'll recheck that dial-in number."

The CEO gave me a look and went right back to reading his email. It didn't seem to faze him at all, but it sure rattled me. I always want to show my professional side, especially during the first few months on a new job.

I turned and quickly headed for my desk to verify the number. I could envision the CEO rolling his eyes as I went through the doorway. I looked at my notes and double-checked the calendar invitation. Sure enough, I had the right number.

I phoned the assistant who sent the meeting invite and learned that she had sent out the wrong dial-in information. I guess I wasn't the only one having an "interesting" day. I could only imagine all the other assistants dialing in and hearing that same sultry voice. What a relief to know that I wasn't alone!

I poked my head inside my executive's office to give him an update. He was focused on his email, so I walked to the phone and dialed the new number and code. Through the speaker, I could hear the other executives who had already joined the call. *Phew!* This time, it was right.

Who knew that dialing a simple conference call could be so entertaining? I got a good laugh from it, although I'm not sure my executive felt the same way. Thank heaven I haven't repeated that mistake again!

WAND
(What Assistants Need Daily)

✳ You will make mistakes. How you recover from them is what makes the difference.

✳ Always double-check telephone numbers to ensure accuracy.

✳ Have a laugh in stressful situations. It will help you keep calm while searching for solutions.

✳ Don't spend time beating yourself up about mistakes. Move on and learn from them.

> A gracious good morning to you. Have I reached the party to whom I am speaking?
>
> **—LILY TOMLIN AS "ERNESTINE THE TELEPHONE OPERATOR"**

Wizards Lead the Way

FIRE DRILL OR REAL EMERGENCY?

Emergency situations always cause emotions to get in the way of reason. To maneuver a difficult situation, sometimes you must own up to bad behavior and be willing to eat humble pie when you're in the wrong.

Working in a small office has its challenges. As the CEO assistant, I didn't have the traditional role. At times, I would be the one signing for FedEx packages, calling a repair person, and contacting building maintenance; in other words, I often wore several hats. One area of responsibility that was delegated to me and our office manager was about safety. Our office suite was on the top floor in a large building. Several other small companies also leased space in the building.

Once a year, one or two employees from each company were required by the property management company to attend a mandatory safety-training meeting. During the hour-long session, we learned about the location of the building exits and where our companies should meet outside the building if there were an incident, the types of alarms that may sound, how to respond, and other relevant topics. We were also given orange safety vests, so our employees would know who was in charge of our floor.

Our employees, including me, weren't excited about hearing the alarm. The idea of being in a burning high-rise caused some anxiety, especially when the alarm sounded. It also meant taking the long walk down several flights of stairs. *Ugh!* I never ran marathons, and my legs could barely do 10,000 steps a day, let alone several flights of stairs. Have you ever tried tackling the stairs in high heels? Trust me: You'd move faster in bare feet.

During one fire drill, a woman from the floor below walked in front of us in super spikey heels. She was walking so slowly that, if the building really had been on fire, our chances of making it out were slim.

I had to hold myself back from shouting, "Take off those *shoes*, woman! This isn't a stroll. A fire alarm is blaring and, for all we know, the building is burning!"

Then it happened. Early one Tuesday morning, one of the alarms sounded. We could only hear it coming from the stairwell; it wasn't sounding on our floor. I started to grab my vest and realized that this alarm was specific to some other floors in our building. If we needed to evacuate, that deafening alarm would have sounded.

I looked down the hallway at the office manager's cube, but she wasn't at her desk. Several executives and staff members were traveling or at other meetings, so only a small number of employees were in the office that day.

I stood up from my cube and confidently said, "Since the alarm is not sounding on our floor, we don't need to evacuate the building. Believe me, if the alarm for the entire building had gone off, we would all know it. The sound is deafening."

I could still hear the faint alarm sounding.

I sat down in my chair, put the vest on my desk, and went back to reviewing emails. Suddenly, some of our staff members came bursting out of a meeting.

"Don't we need to evacuate the building? The fire alarm is sounding. We need to get out now!"

I replied in a seemingly uncaring tone. "We don't need to evacuate. Our floor alarm isn't going off."

I could see the shocked look and frustration in their faces.

One of them responded, "Well, I certainly don't feel safe in this building if *any* alarm is going off."

She continued down the hall, insisting that everyone get up and immediately head for the stairs. People were confused. They weren't sure what to do or who was in charge. Should they stay? Should they go? *What should they do?*

"Everyone, out!" she insisted. "We must evacuate *now*."

She began pulling people out of conference rooms, and even the office manager was rushed into the stairwell with the other employees.

As they headed for the stairs, I shouted, "You're all wasting your time. You'll have to walk down several flights of stairs for no reason. That alarm is not for us. You can all go if you want, but I'm staying here."

Now people were even more confused. Why wouldn't I want to go with them to safety? They all headed for the stairs. I didn't budge.

One of our assistants insisted that I play it safe and take the long walk down the stairs.

"No!" I said with disdain. "Why won't anyone *listen* to me? I've been trained, and this alarm isn't of any concern to us."

By now, we could hear the fire truck pulling up to the building with blaring sirens. The assistant insisted I go with her and wouldn't leave without me.

"Your husband would never forgive me if I left you behind during a fire. Let's not take any chances."

I kicked off my heels and stomped to the stairs with an exasperated attitude. I didn't wear any socks that day, so kicking off those heels meant that I was walking in bare feet. I don't know what's worse: going down the dirty cement stairs in bare feet or walking in heels. Next time, I won't take off my shoes unless the building really *is* burning down!

As we made the long walk down the stairs, I realized that we didn't follow protocol. I was not wearing my orange vest, although I was carrying it in my hand. Most importantly, we didn't clear the floor to make sure that all employees had been evacuated. If it were a real emergency, we may have left coworkers behind. That thought left me with an awful feeling.

As we got to the last step, I heard one of the building staff people say that it was a false alarm. It only impacted three floors, and it didn't include our floor. After hearing that, something inside me wanted to announce to the world that I was right. I just couldn't let it go.

Before I got to our team, I blurted out, "See? I *told* you guys that you'd be wasting your time. We didn't have to leave."

By now, my leg muscles were burning. Boy, was I out of shape!

What was I thinking? I certainly was more concerned about being right than the safety of our team. That wasn't like me to get irritated over something so critical. It bothered me all day.

As we headed for the elevator to return to the office, one of the executives made a comment about what she thought was my inappropriate behavior. Apparently, I had upset her as she was more focused on the safety of the employees than wasting time walking down the stairs. She called me on it. I probably wouldn't have been bothered by her comment except she mentioned it just as we were getting into the elevator to go back up to the office. Everyone could hear her.

Had she done this when we got back in the office and pulled me into a conference room, I believe I would have been more responsive, but she didn't. She decided that it needed to be handled right then. She pulled me aside in the lobby area and proceeded to grill me as to why I was so upset. I must admit that she caught me off guard. Who did she think she was—ordering me around like she was the boss of me? Not only was I embarrassed, now I was angry. Even though I insisted that I was right about the situation, she insisted that *she* was right.

We saw the building management lead and walked over to her for more clarification. Although I was right about how the situation should have been handled, I was wrong in the way I behaved. Yet, I was still *very* irritated about the whole thing.

I turned to head back to the elevator. At least I made it before she could join me. I was too upset to have a calm conversation, especially in the elevator.

She arrived back to the office and went into her meeting. She passed by my desk and avoided looking my way.

"Oh, great," I thought.

I certainly didn't want to cause an awkward situation. I was a little worried that I had compromised our great relationship. Within the hour, I saw an email from her. It was clear that she was feeling the same way.

I can handle all kinds of stressful situations; however, these situations tend to cause me some anxiety. This was a great example of a critical and an awkward conversation. I teach these concepts, which means that I should know what to do and say. When emotions are mixed with these scenarios, it's hard to focus on the facts. Obviously, I let my emotions take over.

On my arrival home that evening, I had a conversation with my husband about my day. From his perspective, he felt that I owed my coworker an apology.

Then he asked, "What are you going to do about it?"

I thought about how I was going to resolve this now awkward situation. It was time to use the techniques I had learned.

I replied to her email by acknowledging that, as far as I was concerned, our relationship was fine. The reason I was so upset was because I really didn't want to walk down several flights of stairs, especially if there wasn't an emergency. I realized later that the other reason was because safety in our office was partly my responsibility. Within seconds of her comments and excitability, it felt as if she took away my authority by shooing everyone into the stairwell while I sat at my desk. When she did that, it caused a lot of confusion for everyone, including me.

This also brought up an excellent point. Our new employees had not been given proper safety training or information about what to do in an emergency. It was time to add that training to our new-hire orientation.

The next day, the two of us had a good conversation. Neither wanted this incident to get in the way of work or our friendship. It is always better when you can separate emotions from the facts, eat a little humble pie, and move on. Friendships are worth it.

Several months after this incident, I went for my annual training. Management reviewed the new procedure: If the fire alarm sounded, we were to evacuate the building regardless of whether it was a blaring alarm. It seems that our exchange with the property manager must have sparked some concern for the tenants' safety, and a new process was implemented. Who knew that conflict between two people could impact a change for the safety of mankind. Safety first!

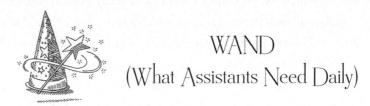

WAND
(What Assistants Need Daily)

❉ Be aware of how your body physically reacts when your emotions kick in. The sooner you're aware of what's happening, the sooner you can control yourself and the situation.

❉ Be sensitive to the needs of those around you in emergency situations. Even though your building may have specific guidelines, if someone doesn't feel safe, they have the right and the choice to go to a safe place.

❉ Have courage and admit when you are wrong or have behaved inappropriately.

❉ There will be times when your ego gets in the way of what's important. Learn to recognize when you're wrong, and don't be afraid to apologize. It can be humbling.

❉ Prepare a document to train new employees about the emergency/safety plan.

✳ Be sure to follow proper safety protocol, especially if you are the one in charge of safety for your department and/or company.

✳ Do not embarrass others in front of their coworkers, regardless of the state of your emotions or your opinion.

✳ If you question a process, procedure, or policy that you feel jeopardizes the safety of others, don't hesitate to bring it to the attention of the proper authorities. If you have a concern, others may feel the same way.

I cannot do confrontation. You know
that fight or flight thing? I'm flight.
I just don't want the argument.

—JENNIFER SAUNDERS

A Wizard's Magic Requires Order

WHO NEEDS AN AGENDA?

Each executive has their own unique style of leadership. At times, they need covert collaboration to help them see that some tools and resources are needed to make a successful team.

One of the executive staff members stopped by my desk after one of their weekly staff meetings and said with exasperation, "I can't take one more meeting like this!"

I looked up from my computer and asked, "How can I help?"

"Our meetings feel like a big waste of time. We never have an agenda, and some of our topics get out of control. In fact, we have one executive who continually hijacks the meeting with his own topics. It could be so much more productive if we just had an agenda."

"I completely understand. We'll have to come up with a plan to help make the situation better."

At other companies, I would help put together the agendas. This CEO was new to the role and, when I first arrived, I asked about his preference in putting together an agenda for his executive staff meetings.

"I don't use agendas, and you certainly don't need to put one together for me. I have it under control." He was inflexible about this process. He wanted full control of his staff meeting details. "Not only do I *not* need an agenda, you don't need to worry about attending either. I'll let you know about any action items that require attention."

As he walked away, I thought, "For such a brilliant man, he still has a lot to learn, especially being a first-time CEO. Perhaps I'm just the one who can help him."

The next week, a few of the executives stopped by my desk again, and the conversation was almost identical: "When will these meetings improve? Why is our CEO against using an agenda?"

I had to do something. I cared for and respected my boss. How could I approach him with such a sensitive matter? I knew how he felt about agendas, but the current format just wasn't working for his team. I didn't think a conversation was the right approach, so I decided to use some creativity.

I emailed the meeting attendees the day before the staff meeting, asking about their priorities and any specific topics to include in the meeting. A few of them responded. With this new information, I put together an *agenda* of my own.

As my boss passed my desk on his way to the staff meeting, I stopped him and took a deep breath.

"I took a survey of the attendees, asking about their top priorities as well as any topics they felt needed to be discussed during the staff meeting. I thought you would be interested to know what's on their minds. I know you don't like agendas, so I've listed the topics in case you want to discuss some of them during your meeting. Even though you may already be aware of this information, I wanted to make sure you were prepared."

He glanced at the agenda with what I thought was a skeptical look. He never touched the paper.

"Thanks," he said with a smile in his eyes. "I appreciate you doing this, but, as I've said, I don't use agendas."

"Got it," I said with compliance, and off to the meeting he went.

As he left my desk, I spun my chair around, put the paper in front of me, and thought, "Aha! This just might work. He actually stopped and looked at the agenda."

Following the meeting, a few of his team members appeared at my desk and said, almost with relief, "Thank you!"

I looked at them and gave a slight chuckle.

They continued. "Thanks for passing along our agenda topics. The CEO covered them in our meeting. It was much more productive. We're very confident that you had something to do with this. How can we keep this up?"

I thought, "He only looked at the paper for a few seconds. How could he possibly have remembered all those items I had listed?"

Little did I know then that he had a photographic memory. It took him only a few seconds to capture everything on the page. All he had to do was look.

I shook myself out of my thoughts and shared my method with them. I promised to do the same for the next meeting.

The following week, I again presented the CEO with my research. As expected, he glanced at the paper and off he went to his meeting. This went on for a few weeks. By the fourth week, the CEO gave me a nice surprise.

"Where's the agenda for our meeting today?" he asked.

Wow! Now he was calling it *the agenda*. Finally, he got it!

He glanced at the list I had gathered, and then said, "Please add these two additional topics," as if this had always been our routine. "After you make the changes, make enough copies for all the staff attendees."

I was speechless.

He quickly glanced at me and added, "Let's plan to do this for every meeting."

"Great idea!" I added with as much enthusiasm as I could muster. I was still in shock from the surprise of it all.

His executives later commented how much more productive the meetings had become.

"There is just one more thing that would make it better," one executive said. "We need someone to hold us accountable. We think it's time for you to attend the meetings and take down the action items."

"I'm not sure our boss will go for that idea."

I was aware that this would be a new level of responsibility, and I was ready for it.

"We'll see about that!" they said as they walked away.

Following the next meeting, my boss appeared at my desk.

"Linda, in our staff meeting today, my entire staff asked if we could have you attend our future meetings. It seems that we're falling short at tracking the action items, especially my own. We'd like you to attend and keep us on track. Will you join us next week?"

I sat up in my chair, looked directly at the CEO, and said, "That's a great idea. Yes, I will attend."

"The staff members trust you. You are a critical member of our team. Not only do we want you to help us keep track of our action items, we want your input too."

I joined the meetings and felt a part of the team during his tenure as CEO. I learned a lot that year about the ups and downs of business, how conflict among leaders can be healthy and productive or counterproductive, and how an assistant can be a critical part of the team.

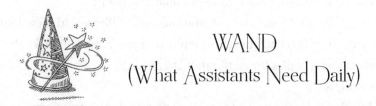

WAND
(What Assistants Need Daily)

✳ Don't be afraid to share your awareness and abilities with others. Even wizards belong to councils to increase their understanding and awareness.

* If you care about the success of your executive, take a risk to share ideas that will improve a process for his/her success as well as the success of the team.

* Don't wait for your executive to give you direction. Be assertive and resourceful. Remember: His/her success reflects on you.

* Find ways to work with your coworkers and department teams. Your ideas can improve productivity and provide valuable insight.

* When you become trustworthy, your team will be more accepting of your input. Build trust by being dependable, honest, and consistent in your behavior.

> Teamwork begins by building trust.
> And the only way to do that is to
> overcome our need for invulnerability.

—PATRICK LENCIONI

Wizards Make Mistakes Too

MURPHY'S LAW AND THE SPECIAL VISA

A long list of things goes wrong while processing a visa. Deadlines were missed and valuable lessons were learned.

D o you ever have one of those projects where, once something goes wrong, it continues to spiral out of control? The CEO and I were finishing up one of our more detailed one-to-one meetings to discuss some urgent items. Near the end, I mentioned that I noticed his special visa would expire within the next few months. There were some changes with the CEO's location, and I wasn't sure if a special business-type visa would still be required.

"I don't think I need that type of visa anymore," he said. "Just in case, I'll send an email to our contact in human resources (HR) to reconfirm. Don't worry about this one," he said while making a note. "I'll let you know if we need to do anything."

I also placed a note in my task "to do" list. I didn't want this issue to be overlooked, especially if our CEO was required to still have a special visa.

Several weeks went by, and I hadn't heard anything more about the visa status. I mentioned it again to the CEO, which triggered a reminder for him too.

"I'll send a follow-up."

He didn't seem concerned, so I didn't push it. However, by this time, I was getting a little anxious. Since I had never processed this type of visa, I wasn't sure what was involved or how long it would take.

A few days later, I received an email from our lawyers who would be assisting with the visa process and documentation. As I read their email, I realized that the CEO would in fact need the visa, and it was quite a complicated process with lots of paperwork. Time was running out! He wouldn't be able to travel to the country for business if we let it lapse. As I reviewed the application, it was obvious that I needed his input to answer many of the questions. My boss was traveling, so I waited.

Upon his return, we reviewed and completed the questions on the application. I submitted it to the lawyers, believing that the document was in their capable hands and would be processed with haste.

A week passed. I erroneously assumed that the visa was already on its way to wherever it needed to go for processing. That wasn't the case. An email appeared in my inbox with several other questions that needed to be addressed.

"I thought we were much farther along in this process!" I exclaimed silently.

My first reaction was panic, then frustration, and then more panic.

I emailed the attorney, writing, "What happens if my boss travels to this country before the application is processed?"

A few days went by and still no word from the attorney. I sent a second email, stressing the urgency as the CEO would be traveling in the next few weeks for some critical meetings.

"We don't recommend that the CEO travel until we are compliant with his visa," stated the lawyers.

What? We had a board meeting scheduled in a few days and were due to announce earnings. Following the earnings call, we had several meetings scheduled with investors. How would we explain the absence of the CEO at these critical meetings?

I quickly completed all the additional paperwork. Surely they knew the urgency of this situation. As it was vacation and holiday season, the timeline seemed to get dragged out. It didn't help that the details were being sent piece by piece instead of receiving all the information at once.

At last, the application was submitted, appointments were scheduled with the embassy, passport photos were taken, and the CEO headed to the embassy in San Francisco to finalize the visa papers. The embassy accepted the documents and advised the CEO that they would send the passport, the visa, and any other documents to the CEO's home address.

Another several days passed. It was now getting close to the Thanksgiving holiday. My boss had some travel plans, so we talked about him using his second passport if his main passport didn't arrive in time. Imagine my relief when he texted the Wednesday before the holiday that the passport had finally arrived!

In his haste, the CEO neglected to mention that there was another document included when the passport and visa were reccived. It described the next steps for processing the visa. Since I didn't have the information, I wasn't aware of this critical step. *Yikes!* We weren't done yet. On entry in the country, the CEO was to present the passport and visa at a specific location at the airport.

After the holiday, I sent a follow-up email to the attorneys, letting them know that we had received the visa.

Within 24 hours, I received a response: "Fantastic news! Now the CEO will just need to present the passport and visa when he arrives, so the visa can be officially stamped within 30 days of the embassy issuing the visa."

Why didn't I have this information? There was no email that advised about the requirement to process the visa within 30 days of being issued. The bad news is that the CEO wasn't scheduled to go to that specific country again until the end of January.

I had a large knot in my stomach. After a few email exchanges, it was clear that we couldn't comply with the 30-day timeframe. What made things even more exasperating is that we were told we had to start the application process all over again. *Seriously?*

I gently broke the news to our CEO.

"Why didn't anyone tell us about this step to get the visa finalized?" he asked.

I knew that his frustration wasn't targeted at me; however, I felt awful that I didn't have the proper information so that this could have been avoided.

I asked him an important question: "By any chance, do you remember receiving a letter or any other documentation when the passport and visa were sent to your home?"

"No. I don't recall receiving any documentation."

"Well, the attorney mentioned that we should have received a letter from the embassy when they processed the visa. That letter, along with your passport and visa, will need to be presented at a designated location when you travel in the country. The documentation is only good for 30 days. That means we have to start the process all over again."

We talked about the second round and were more aware of what to expect. I emailed the attorneys to make sure that our timing would work. I also asked them to please share any additional tasks that we would need to know to complete the process. Receiving bits and pieces of the information instead of all the details was really frustrating.

I started the process all over again. This time, I pushed things through and constantly followed up to ensure we had a date with the embassy that coincided with my CEO's travel in order to be compliant with the 30-day time period.

The date arrived, and my CEO presented his passport. Then I learned that processing the visa would take seven to 10 days, and the CEO would have to pick it up in person at a post office near our corporate office. Why didn't anyone tell us this while we were going through the process? Trying to start all over again was unthinkable! Unfortunately, the CEO was only scheduled to be in the country for five days—not seven to 10 days! What steps did we need to take to make sure he had his passport in hand before he departed?

A few of our staff members, who were located in this country, were helping with the process and had some connections. A few calls were made to see if we could put a priority request on the processing as our CEO had some pressing matters outside the country. He needed his passport in order to keep his commitments.

I worked on a backup plan in case the special visa didn't come through. The only thing left to do was wait, and thank heaven we didn't have to wait long. The CEO received a call that his passport and special visa were ready for pickup. They reminded him that he had to pick up the documents in person. No staff member was allowed to pick up the document on his behalf. He received the call and arranged for a pickup of the passport just in time to make the flight that was scheduled the next morning. With passport and special visa in hand, the CEO was off to the airport with all the paperwork in order.

This experience taught me a generous lesson about thinking ahead and not being shy about asking questions, especially when you're doing something for the first time.

WAND
(What Assistants Need Daily)

☀ When you make mistakes, spot them, learn from them, and fix them.

☀ When handling a project or process for the first time, make a list of questions to ask and document the answers. Include questions you believe may be stupid.

☀ Brainstorm ideas to help see every possible solution.

☀ Keep information, resources, and questions you gathered along the way. You never know when you may be asked to do a similar project in the future.

☀ If you are unsure if paperwork needs to be processed, push to get information. The last thing you want is for your boss to get stuck in customs or somewhere worse.

In any field of endeavor, anything that
can go wrong, will go wrong.
—MURPHY'S LAW

Wizards Entice Transformation

TRAVEL POINTS ANYONE?

With a little ingenuity and experience, along with an idea and process used at previous companies, a simple change in tracking corporate travel points saves the company $100,000 the first year.

I was consumed with an upcoming trip for my CEO when I was unexpectedly interrupted by one of our human resource staff members.

"Do you have a minute?" she asked with concern in her voice.

"Sure. What's up?" I was curious to find out what was causing her anxiety.

"One of our directors recently left the company. While we were cleaning out his desk and reviewing his email, we found a stack of travel certificates and information about travel points for our company travelers. Most of the certificates were going to expire in a few months. It seemed that he was designated as the person to control travel points and certificates for our U.S. travelers. No one really knew how he became the designated 'travel manager' for the United States. We've done some checking, and we can't find any official process. We've asked around, and some of the assistants in the office knew that the director had certificates and points. They would use them from time to time but not on a regular basis. It seems that we never set up an official process or communicated to the travelers, leaving the certificates and points unused most of the time. After talking with our HR team, we were wondering if you could take over this responsibility for now. No one else even has a clue of what to do. Can you help?"

Oh, boy. The last thing I needed was more responsibility. Plus, what did I know about putting together any type of process or program using points and certificates for travelers? That was *not* my area of expertise.

"Why me?" I responded with immense apprehension. "I may know how to do complicated travel for executives, but I don't know the first thing about putting something like this together. Are you sure this is something you want me to handle?"

I came to the conclusion that they must be desperate to reach out to me. We didn't have a dedicated travel manager at the time for the U.S. travelers. I suppose I should have taken it as a compliment, but I believed the HR department didn't want to handle it. Honestly, why would they?

I responded with a curious attitude, saying, "Shouldn't this responsibility belong to finance or the travel manager?"

"Well, we don't have anyone in our U.S. finance department who can handle this, and our travel manager is located in another country. Would you consider taking over this program at least for the next few months?"

I have a hard time saying "no" to these types of requests. I love solving problems, but did I really have time for this?

Then I remembered something about how our travel policy, points, and certificates had been managed at a few previous companies where I had worked.

"Yes. I'll take it on. I have an idea."

I'm pretty sure the HR staff member was relieved to know that I had agreed to take on the project. In one minute, I was giving excuses as to why I didn't want to take it on; in the next minute, I was enthusiastically volunteering to manage the program! In any case, they were happy to send it my way, and I had the details in no time.

At previous companies, the travel agency had always managed the travel points and certificates program. Why wouldn't our current travel agency provide the same service? They must have some type of tracking system for travelers to use points and certificates.

I called my contact, who handled the program for our executive staff members. I was hoping she could point me in the right direction. I explained my situation and included details about the type of program needed. Imagine my excitement when she answered "yes" and provided a quick summary of the program!

After several conversations, email exchanges, and discussions with our travel manager to provide her expertise, a program was established. Details were communicated to our travelers, and the program was officially launched just a few weeks later.

I was so happy! Instead of having responsibility for a new project, the travel agency would manage the program, and we'd have a great way for travelers to save money. It just made sense. Who better to handle our travelers' needs than the agency that had all the information and view into our corporate travel details? The added bonus was that the travel agency would also track the savings and provide a monthly report to our finance department.

About a year later, I was putting together my self-evaluation for my performance review and remembered the travel program idea and launch. I reached out to my contact at the travel agency to see if she could send a report showing how much money the new program had saved the company over the past year. She didn't hesitate to tell me the good news: That year, the program had saved the company over $100,000. In fact, the company had already saved over $35,000 for the first three months of the new year.

I quickly added the information to my self-evaluation and hoped that this program's success would have a generous raise awaiting.

WAND
(What Assistants Need Daily)

✳ Dazzle others with your transformational ideas through experience, logic, and a little mystery.

✳ Use your ingenuity. It can go a long way.

✳ Don't be afraid to share your ideas and help implement new programs, especially when it means a savings to the company.

✳ Don't overlook opportunities that may come your way. It may not always mean extra work. It might be a valuable use of your creative ideas and experience.

✳ When others think of you to help with projects, take it as a compliment. They value your input and work ethic.

> First comes thought; then organization
> of that thought, into ideas and plans;
> then transformation of those plans
> into reality. The beginning, as you will
> observe, is in your imagination.
>
> —NAPOLEON HILL

Wizards Are Rarely Caught Off Guard

THE CASE OF THE MISSING EMAIL

Sometimes even the CEO makes a mistake and needs to eat a little humble pie.

I scurried to my desk. It was one of those Mondays where I was already behind and a little late to the office.

My boss was in focus mode. He was anxious for me to arrive as there were several pressing priorities, and one in particular was on his mind. Before I could get settled, he asked if I had a chance to set up a meeting for one of his more pressing topics. Apparently, over the weekend he had sent a detailed email with some specific action items.

My son and his family had been visiting from out of town, and checking email wasn't on my radar. I wanted to spend every minute with my grandchildren. Visiting the zoo, going to the park, and dancing to their favorite songs were my priorities that weekend. Although I often check, I had scanned my inbox and didn't see any pressing matters. Since my boss had mentioned a specific email even before I had a chance to sit down, I quickly reviewed the hundreds of emails that had piled up over the past few days, scanning for that topic.

"I have a lot of email right now," I said to my boss. "To help move things along, tell me who needs to be in the meeting and the subject I should use for the invite."

In my CEO's rush to get the item on the schedule, he gave me a quick overview along with the key attendees to be included. Although I still hadn't seen the email in my inbox, I decided to set up the meeting and look for the details later. I got lucky, and all of the attendees were available the following day. Now I could check *that* item off my list!

I worked my way through the emails, trying to prioritize all of the requests. I still didn't see the one from my boss and, because of that, I wasn't sure that I had all the correct details. Was I losing my mind, or was it the lack of sleep from having visitors all weekend? Luckily, I had access to my executive's inbox, so I decided to look at his sent folder to find the missing email.

As I scrolled through the sent emails, one in particular stood out. It had the exact subject line of the project that my boss had been asking about.

"Strange," I thought. "I haven't seen this email, so I'd better take a quick look."

Sure enough, there was the email with all the details! I checked to see if I was copied. I inspected the addresses and saw my name. I scratched my head, wondering how I had missed this, and then I saw the reason: The letter "o" had been left out of ".com," so the email never arrived in my inbox.

I couldn't believe my eyes. For a boss who *never* wants *me* to make a mistake, here was a doozy from him. Do I take the high road or bring it to his attention? I knew he had lots of pressing matters on his mind, so timing needed to be perfect. This time, I wasn't going to let it go. I thought I'd have a little fun.

He came back to his desk after getting a cup of coffee.

"I figured out why I was confused about the urgent email," I said with some levity in my voice. "Since I couldn't find it in my inbox, I took a look in yours, and there it was: the mysterious email. My detective skills paid off. I know you think you copied me, but, believe it or not, you made a typo in my email address."

It was obvious that he didn't believe me. He was a type-A personality, someone who rarely acknowledged his mistakes but never hesitated to let me know when I made one. He immediately pulled up the email to have a closer look.

"I can't *believe* it! I *do* have a typo. No wonder you were confused."

I just smiled, mentally blew the smoke off my magic wand, and put it back in its sheath.

WAND
(What Assistants Need Daily)

✻ Like wizards, strive for excellence in your work. Coworkers will learn to appreciate your high work ethic.

✻ If there is confusion about an email, don't jump to conclusions. Use your detective skills.

✻ Use humor only when appropriate. Timing is everything.

✻ Learn to be aware of your executive's style. It can help you better understand their behavior.

✻ Set boundaries, as needed, to ensure that you have time to rest as well as time to spend with family and friends.

> Excellence is the gradual result of
> always striving to do better.
>
> —PAT RILEY

About the Author

L inda McFarland brings her consummate professionalism, calm demeanor, and insightful sense of humor to her highly acclaimed presentations and workshops. Having supported over a dozen CEOs in Silicon Valley, Linda shares her decades of experience through stories that bring out the thoughtful lessons learned throughout her career. Her passion for sharing her knowledge and understanding with other assistants led her to launch a consulting company—Ascend2Success—to develop educational and interactive training for assistants, event planners, and other support professionals.

MORE ABOUT LINDA

❊ Executive assistant to CEOs in Silicon Valley, supporting over a dozen CEOs and spanning the medical, energy, and high-technology industries

❊ Former chair and current advisory board member for Silicon Valley Admin Awards, the first and only awards program of its kind in the country that publicly recognizes the invaluable contributions of assistants

❊ Active and founding member of the Silicon Valley Catalysts Association, a group for CEO assistants in Silicon Valley

❊ Along with a team of CEO assistants and UCSC Extension of Silicon Valley, helped develop the first certificate program for assistants; former advisory board member, master instructor, and guest lecturer

❊ Former cofounder of Admin to Admin

❊ Coauthored the book, *Sitting on a File Cabinet, Naked, with a Gun: True Stories of Silicon Valley CEO Assistants*

✳ Guest speaker at corporate events and conferences

✳ Certified trainer for Office Dynamics—Star Achievement Series®

✳ Former cofounder of PlanetAdmin, a training company for assistants

✳ Founded McFarland Consulting, which was the beginning of Linda's consulting career

✳ Married with four children and several grandchildren

54976909R00080

Made in the USA
Middletown, DE
14 July 2019